educate to self-regulate

empowering learners for lifelong success

DR SHYAM BARR

Praise for *Educate to Self-Regulate*

'This book is an excellent handbook as we continue to seamlessly embed SRL into our teaching practice.'
Louise Wallace-Richards, Assistant Principal Teaching and Learning, Radford College

'Shyam has laid out a rich bed of research, theory and on-the-ground practice that is distilled in a practical way.'
Dipesh Vadher, Head of Science, The King David School

'The evidence-based step-by-step advice not only resonated with my experiences but challenged me to reconsider my own learning.'
Tegan Knuckey, Assistant Principal, Balwyn High School

'This insightful book balances current research-informed insights with teacher classroom experiences.'
Alison Easey, Deputy Principal (Learning and Teaching), Burgmann Anglican School

'I encourage motivated practitioners to read Shyam's book with both their own learning and that of their students in mind.'
Catherine Misson, Strategy, Leadership and Culture Consultant, Past Principal, and Principal Emeritus

'Dr Barr's work is a must-read, bridging the gap between theory and practice.'
Dr Luke Mandouit, Vice-Principal, Geelong Grammar School

'This book should be an essential part of teacher and school leadership training.'
Mathew Green, Host of *The Art of Teaching* podcast and Assistant Principal

'This book is an exceptional offering to the professional learning space for educators.'
Marc Warwick, Deputy Principal, ACT Education Directorate

'Dr Barr's book is a transformative manual for educators. A must-read offering a timely shift towards empowering students.'
Ian Tilbury, Deputy Headteacher (Teaching, Learning and Curriculum), The Astley Cooper School

'Shyam's balance of research and practical examples makes this an essential read for all educators.'
Greg Terrell, Principal, Bonython Primary School

'*Educate to Self-Regulate* gives educators the knowledge and practical tools to support the future-proofing of our students.'
Amanda Hawkins, Deputy Principal, Bonython Primary School

'This book provides the evidence base and structured approach I've been looking for to encourage my students to value their learning process over product.'
Meg Brydon, Director of VCE and Data, Melbourne Girls Grammar

'A must-read for educators, parents and individuals seeking practical strategies for personal and professional growth.'
Mark Moule, Casual Relief Teacher, ANZUK

'A must-read for teachers who need a roadmap to implement teaching of SRL.'
Dr Patrick Sins, Professor of Learning, Rotterdam University of Applied Sciences

'Shy's book provides evidence-informed strategies for teaching SRL, and unpacks the theory in sensible, digestible bites.'
Kim Brady, Leader of Teaching and Learning, Novo Education Space

'This book addresses an important gap in the literature on SRL.'
Robin Irvine, Learning Designer, Swinburne University, Australia

'*Educate to Self-Regulate* guides readers through the process of becoming a self-regulated learner and educating others in this profound process.'
Max Woods, Founder and Creator, ALARM Education

'Shyam has masterfully clarified the complexities of SRL and provided a comprehensive, practical and transferable set of reflections and resources.'
Andrew Herft, Curriculum Advisor

'The academic underpinnings of this book give it such gravitas and depth, without detracting from the practicality and accessibility.'
Kath Murdoch, Author and International Education Consultant

*This book is dedicated to our young people,
including my children – Marlow and Ziggy.*

*May you experience an education that supports you
to develop a strong learner identity and the skill set
to self-regulate your learning for life.*

Published in 2024 by Amba Press, Melbourne, Australia
www.ambapress.com.au

© Shyam Barr 2024

The moral rights of the author have been asserted.

All rights reserved. No part of this book may be reproduced or transmitted in any form or by any means, electronic or mechanical, including photocopying, recording or by any information storage and retrieval system, without prior permission in writing from the publisher.

Cover design: Tess McCabe
Internal design: Amba Press
Editor: Brooke Lyons

ISBN: 9781923116559 (pbk)
ISBN: 9781923116566 (ebk)

A catalogue record for this book is available from the National Library of Australia.

Contents

Acknowledgements	ix
Foreword	xi
Introduction	1

Part I: Foundations of SRL — 11

1	Why teach SRL?	15
2	What is SRL, really?	26

Part II: Instructional approaches for developing SRL — 47

3	Identifying students' SRL level	51
4	Explicit teaching approaches to promote SRL	67
5	Incorporating SRL instruction into curriculum design	80
6	Pedagogies to enhance metacognition for SRL	97
7	A positive classroom climate for SRL	115

Part III: Leading an SRL school improvement initiative — 127

8	Assessing SRL: Competency-based learning approaches	129
9	Assessing SRL: Questionnaires, focus groups and online traces	145
10	Exploring teachers' SRL knowledge, beliefs and practice	157
11	Launching a whole-school SRL initiative	167

Conclusion	183
References	187
About the author	193

Acknowledgements

Country

My journey in writing this book has found me on many lands and countries. However, the large portion of this book was written on Wurundjeri Country (Melbourne, Victoria) and Ngunnawal Country (Canberra, Australian Capital Territory). As I write this acknowledgement, I can see ancient trees spotted among rooftops, the big eucalyptus tree outside my office window, and a range of birds from cockatoos to rosellas visiting. The soft green of the leaves brings me a sense of calm and a level of clarity that has allowed me to put these words on paper. Here, I express my deepest gratitude to the traditional custodians of this land, those who have cared for, and those who continue to care for, this beautiful country – Australia. Thank you.

Support and contributions

I would also like to acknowledge Amba Press, particularly Alicia Cohen for her unwavering support and hustle in helping me publish this book; and Kelly Irving and the Expert Author Community for their guidance on all aspects of the book writing journey. To the educators who reviewed my book (multiple times) and shared valuable feedback that helped craft this book: my deepest gratitude. I'm a big believer of 'get feedback early, get feedback often', so thank you.

To the many amazing educators that I work with daily, thank you for your continued inspiration, the encouragement to write a book, and the many questions that we continue to generate about teaching SRL. Specifically, I would like to acknowledge Radford College (ACT), Dickson College (ACT), Bonython Primary School (ACT) and staff at Melbourne Girls Grammar (Vic) for collaborating with me to explore approaches for fostering SRL in classrooms and schools and their continued commitment to fostering students' SRL.

Lastly, my family: without your belief in my capability and mission, this book would not have become a reality. To my wife, Reahn Barr, thank you for supporting me and our family throughout this whole process. To my mother, Marian Jansen, thank you for instilling a love of learning in me from such a young age. To my children, Marlow and Ziggy, thank you for being my daily reminder of the importance of my work in this world, and for our young people.

You – the reader

To you – the reader – a leader, a teacher, a parent… In a world where there is so much competing for our attention and time, I am deeply grateful to you for picking up this book. It's symbolic of the value you place on SRL and your investment in our young people – our future.

Foreword

Very few researchers manage to put their research findings into practice. Even if you put your heart and soul into researching a topic, it is often difficult to translate the results of your research in such a way that practitioners can use them and understand their relevance. This is often due to the fact that different languages are spoken in educational research and educational practice, and the needs of practitioners are often not heard in research. As a result, research findings remain abstract and seem to have little relevance for school practice – despite the fact that they could often be highly important.

This equally applies to the field of self-regulated learning (SRL). Over the past two decades, we have gained exciting insights into how SRL can improve and facilitate the learning of students of all ages, with and without learning difficulties, in individual work, group work or classroom settings. We now have concrete answers to the questions of how SRL can be promoted in the classroom, and how to support the development of students' SRL. Nevertheless, very few of us have so far managed to anchor our research findings in school practice. I know of no other colleague who applies the findings of SRL research to practitioners in the school context in such a practical, accessible, convincing and sensitive way as Dr Shyam Barr does.

We urgently need accessible, understandable and engaging information on SRL that is prepared for teachers. Not only to introduce educators in the teaching profession to the topic, but to prepare prospective teachers during their studies and training. So I would like to thank Shyam not only for the invitation to write this foreword, but for writing this great book, which fills a gap that we have had in SRL research for so long.

This book answers the question of how SRL can be optimally promoted in educational settings. It first explains why SRL is relevant for learning and why SRL does not occur spontaneously. The most up-to-date and comprehensive research findings are used to present the concept of what SRL actually is.

Appropriate examples of learning and teaching situations are given at every point in the book. Strategies for educators to assess and adaptively support SRL in learners are presented in concrete terms. In the process, assessment tools that we have developed and validated in SRL research are broken down so that educators can use them directly in their lessons. Shyam uses the latest research findings to develop a highly applied model (NEMO-T), providing teachers with concrete recommendations for action to support and advance the development of their students' SRL. The important concept of metacognition and its role in SRL is also introduced. In addition to the explicit promotion of SRL and the use of SRL strategies, the book also provides a good overview of how teachers can design their lessons to indirectly promote and activate SRL.

In the last two chapters, Shyam makes a plea for the professionalisation of teachers on this topic. For educators, learning about SRL involves more than the mere transfer of knowledge. It is not enough to understand what SRL is – educators need to develop a deep belief that SRL helps their students. They should feel able to promote SRL in their teaching. To do this, they need more than specialist knowledge – they need the conviction and motivational orientation that SRL helps pupils and that it can be learned, and they need practical tools to adapt to their classroom. Just as the theory of SRL profoundly assumes that SRL processes are always constructivist processes in which learners adopt agency, the learning of educators about SRL is also a coconstructivist process in which educators become agents for their teaching and for their promotion of SRL.

In my view, this book covers all aspects that are necessary to give SRL a place in school practice and to inspire educators to become enthusiastic about SRL. I will make this book mandatory reading in all the courses I teach in teacher education and will give it as a gift to all teachers who invest their valuable time to contribute to our research studies. I have been waiting for this book for a long time!

I hope this book achieves the goal that Shyam clearly had in mind when writing it: to get educators as excited about SRL as we are about SRL research. I hope you enjoy reading it – I am sure it will be a most valuable investment of your time!

Dr Charlotte Dignath
Professor for Educational Psychology
Institute of Psychology
Goethe University Frankfurt (Germany)

Introduction

> To maintain job relevance and support future career transitions in a world with artificial intelligence, individuals will require highly developed self-regulated learning skills.
> — Markauskaite et al. (2022, p. 3)

Our current job landscape is changing rapidly with enhanced technology, artificial intelligence (AI) and a proliferation of information due to globalisation. Jobs that require routine tasks are being replaced, compelling the current workforce to engage in an ongoing process of upskilling, or risk unemployment. Upskilling requires high-level learning skills that enable one to adapt and innovate in response to new demands and changing circumstances, a skill set known as self-regulated learning (SRL).

> *SRL is the capability to understand your own thinking, motivations, emotions and behaviours in the context of learning, and to monitor and change these in response to a problem or towards a desired goal.*

Being able to self-regulate as a learner has risen to the top of the 'skills in demand' list. For example, the World Economic Forum (2021, p. 14) listed 'active learning and learning strategies' as number two in its 'Global Top 5 Skills of 2025' (analytical thinking and innovation came in at number one). In the World Economic Forum's 2023 *Future of Jobs Report*, SRL is covered within the top ten skills on the rise ('curiosity and lifelong learning' is listed as number four, while 'motivation and self-awareness' is number ten). In a collaborative study, a group of leading authors in the field of AI were asked the question: 'What kind of capabilities do people need in a world with AI?'. Dragan Gasevic (Professor of Learning Analytics, Monash University) indicated SRL as the number 1 capability due to:

> *(i) the need to adapt (re- or up-skill) frequently due to speed of job and life changes; and (ii) the need to maintain agency in decision making while working AI systems. (Markauskaite et al., 2022, p. 3.)*

SRL is a skill set that empowers students to engage in learning more actively. For learners, this means being keenly aware of how they think and what they feel about the material they're learning. It's about recognising when they're motivated or when their attention starts to wane. Students who are adept at SRL can notice when they're struggling with a concept and then use strategies to overcome these challenges. They might adjust their approach, try new study techniques or seek help when needed. SRL also involves setting clear goals and tracking progress towards them, allowing students to steer their learning in a direction that aligns with their aspirations and academic requirements. In essence, SRL equips students with a mental toolkit to not just cope with educational challenges but to excel through them by self-managing their thoughts, feelings and actions in a way that fosters effective learning.

To help you further understand the concept of SRL, I ask you to imagine that there is a living room in your mind:

In this living room, the TV is mostly on. It's showing your thinking – your thoughts. At times, you may feel so immersed in the TV that you feel like you're one with the television. You are your thoughts. Other times, you're able to separate yourself from the TV – watching your thoughts, the 'TV show', as if sitting on a metaphorical couch. In this instance, you might say that you're the observer – you're noticing your thoughts. Now imagine you've just discovered the remote and can change the channel. You're self-regulating your thinking, changing its course – in this case, for learning. Each button on the remote represents a different tool, a different learning strategy (Barr, 2022a).

I introduced the 'living room of the mind' metaphor in my TEDx Talk about the importance of teaching SRL. Watch my TEDx Talk: **shyambarr.com.au/book**

In the living room of the mind metaphor, the different levels of SRL are as depicted in Figure 1.

The role of education, with teachers at the helm, is to support and nurture the development of an SRL skill set in students, that primes them for success beyond the classroom walls. As demonstrated in Figure 1, this includes developing an awareness of ourselves as learners (observing the TV) and having access to a repertoire of strategies and the knowledge to apply these strategies in different learning contexts (the remote). By integrating SRL into your teaching, you empower students to become adept at managing their own learning processes, which is essential for adapting to the unpredictable challenges of the future.

Figure 1. SRL: the living room of the mind

TV

Thinking

Sitting on the couch watching the TV

Noticing your thinking

Using the remote to change the channel on the TV

Self-regulation

Three SRL opportunities

As an educator, you want your students to develop this skill set so they can do well at school and beyond. But, as you wander the room mid-lesson, you can't help but feel an overwhelming sense of concern. *How will these students manage their learning in the real world when they can barely manage their learning in the classroom?*

You might be noticing a pattern of unproductive learning behaviours. For instance:

- Students are distracted by their friends, laptops and phones.
- Students lack motivation and engagement.
- Echoing claims that 'This is too hard!' and 'I can't do this; I don't know how.'
- The quality of students' writing declining over time, suggesting an inability to organise their thoughts and knowledge.
- A general lack of awareness in students of themselves as learners and their capability to articulate their learning process.
- A perceived unwillingness to take advantage of extra support options (such as early draft submissions and feedback or lunchtime help).
- Over-compliance – students so reliant on instruction that you question their ability to think for themselves and actively participate in the learning process.

Given your learners' challenges in developing their SRL skills, you might find yourself falling into a deficit view – potentially stuck in the problem box that your students are just not able to self-regulate as learners. To counter this feeling, I reframe these challenges as a set of key educational opportunities.

Opportunity 1: Students can better understand themselves as learners and their learning processes

It is widely acknowledged that for students to self-regulate their learning, they require knowledge of their thinking, encompassing the cognitive processes of how information is processed, including encoding, storage and retrieval. They must also be aware of the strengths and limitations of their attention span, along with the various cognitive biases that can influence their thought processes.

A more holistic view on SRL is that students also benefit from a deep understanding of their motivation, emotion and how to effectively manage different resources (such as time and help-seeking). It's not only about knowing the *how* to self-regulate their learning but also recognising the *can* – that they are indeed capable of regulating their learning process. Some students may not realise it's even possible for them to take control of their learning journey. This realisation is separate from the knowledge of how to enact such regulation.

Once a student is cognisant of their learning process, they can better identify when obstacles hinder thinking and learning.

Opportunity 2: Students can develop a repertoire of effective strategies to regulate their thinking or behaviours

As well as understanding learning processes, students with a repertoire of effective strategies are more capable of self-regulating their learning. For example, when a learner understands how they think and can notice when they are experiencing low self-efficacy (lacking belief in their ability to execute the behaviours to successfully complete a task), they might activate a suitable strategy such as reflecting on previous successes or seeking verbal encouragement to boost their self-efficacy.

With a deeper knowledge of effective SRL strategies, learners can more effectively navigate obstacles that emerge in their learning journey. The aim is for students to possess a broad range of strategies in their toolbelts so that if one strategy fails, they can choose another to help progress learning.

Opportunity 3: Students can deliberately practise SRL in the classroom

Once students are well-equipped for SRL – they have a sound understanding of their cognitive processes and have strategies to regulate their learning – they need opportunities to deliberately practice self-regulation. Many school structures and teaching approaches focus on external regulation, where the teacher or school regulates students' learning. However, for students to become effective self-regulated learners, they require opportunities to internally regulate their learning. This requires a shift in lesson design and school structures to allow for appropriate scaffolding of SRL (we'll discuss this in Part II of this book), combined with greater autonomy and choice in learning. My advice is not to remove all support structures, but to adopt the often-used 'gradual release of responsibility' approach (externally regulated to co-regulated to self-regulated) that allows students to achieve greater independence in their learning. The level of autonomy required will vary from student to student.

Our role as educators is to help our learners realise these opportunities and the benefits that follow. Indeed, education research has long demonstrated that SRL skills can be taught, and SRL interventions are highly effective. Many studies provide compelling evidence of intervention impact, where effect sizes of 0.2 are considered small, 0.5 medium and 0.8 large (Cohen, 1992). For example, Dignath et al. (2008) reported an effect size of 0.69, indicating that approximately 75.5 per cent of students receiving SRL instruction outperformed their peers in control groups on learning tests. This aligns with findings from Donker et al. (2014), who consolidated 58 studies and found a similar effect size of 0.66, highlighting the benefits of SRL interventions across educational levels. More recently, Elhusseini et al. (2022) published a comprehensive meta-analysis that reviewed 46 peer-reviewed studies from the past five decades. The findings indicated that SRL interventions had a positive overall effect on academic outcomes, including reading, writing and maths performance, for both children and adolescents.

Depending on where you are in your teaching and learning journey will influence how you utilise this book in your teaching practice and with your students.

For example, if you are relatively new to the field of SRL, then perhaps you feel like you don't know what SRL is or have the confidence to effectively support young people with their SRL. You might be asking:

- What is SRL… really?
- Why is it so important?
- How do I begin to teach it?

Or perhaps you're an experienced teacher, relatively well-established in your practice but aware of the opportunities and carry a desire to ensure that your practice stays contemporary and is informed by the latest research in the field. You might be asking:

- Is SRL still what I think it is?
- What does the latest research say about how to promote SRL in classrooms?
- How might I tweak/enhance my practice so that I can continue to best serve my students?

Or you might be a school leader, interested in exploring how you can integrate SRL more seamlessly into teaching and learning. You might be asking:

- How do I implement a school approach for SRL?
- Where do I start?
- What are the quality indicators?
- Where does the assessment and reporting of SRL fit?

No matter the entry point, this book distils the latest research into a guide, helping you establish or deepen your understanding of SRL, and most importantly *how* to help your students to better self-regulate their learning, with the intention of empowering them for lifelong success. By taking the time to deeply process the learning offered in this book and apply it in your classroom and school, you can feel confident that your practice is informed by the latest educational research and your students have the best chance of developing this essential skill set.

A carefully crafted reading experience

This book was born out of 17 years of professional experience in the education sector, working as a teacher, leader, researcher and advisor in various teaching and learning contexts, both nationally and internationally.

Many educators term me an 'expert' in teaching SRL, based on my extensive formal qualifications, including two master's degrees (one in educational leadership, policy and change, the second in cognitive psychology and educational practice) and a PhD awarded in 2021. This perception is compounded by my current work as a Professional Associate of the University of Canberra, previously an Assistant Professor of Learning Sciences. Through my varying roles, I have conducted and disseminated research on professional learning approaches that support teachers' thinking and practice about SRL and have won several awards and recognition, celebrating the quality of my research, teaching and school partnerships.

Personally, I prefer the term 'specialist' – given my deep interest in understanding SRL and my commitment to continue to develop my understanding and practice in this field. I see this not as work, but as my mission – to help educators foster students' SRL, enabling young people to bring about their preferred future. My involvement in various forms of communication, whether it's recording a podcast or YouTube video, writing a blog, journal article or, in this case, authoring a book, – are all vital endeavours towards fulfilling this mission. This fervent interest and sense of purpose propel my engagement with SRL, through research studies and extensive conversations with educational leaders, teachers, and students. It's all aimed at gathering insights to optimally support you and the young people under your guidance.

In this book, I'll help you identify what is getting in the way of your students' SRL, or to move closer to your aspirations for students. This book is a guide to applying evidence-informed teaching approaches that can support your students' SRL progress in your classroom and across your school. I sincerely hope that you and your students benefit from the learning that I offer here.

I have written the book with several important points in mind, which I will outline in the following sections.

Connecting to your professional knowledge and experience

As mentioned, I recognise that you might be picking up this book with many years of teaching experience, perhaps exceeding my own. Nothing that I share here is intended to diminish your knowledge, experience or professional decisions to date. I respect your wealth of knowledge and suspect many of you are already teaching SRL or aspects of SRL, therefore, this book is a dynamic resource to enhance your already existing practice. I only hope to contribute to a conversation about how *we*, as educators, can best support our young people to develop as self-regulated learners. I trust that you will critically consider the information in light of your professional stance and within your context.

Towards evidence-informed practice

This book bridges the often-daunting gap between theory and practice, a critical step in supporting you as an evidence-informed practitioner. By meticulously blending research findings with practical classroom experience,

I offer a clear, application-focused roadmap for teachers. As you delve into these pages, you'll notice that the references chosen are not just a random collection from an exhaustive literature review. Instead, they have been carefully selected for their direct relevance and benefit. Each one plays a pivotal role in helping to communicate key points and insights, ensuring that the theoretical foundations laid down are not just informative but also practically applicable in real classroom settings. This approach underpins my commitment to not only inform but also empower teachers with research-backed strategies, ensuring that the teaching profession continues to be strongly positioned as an evidence-informed profession.

Emerging questions

As you read this book, please keep in mind that my knowledge of SRL is evolving daily and this is a snapshot of my current understanding of the field and the way that it relates to practice. Please take note of any reflections and questions that emerge for you as you read. Discuss the questions with your colleagues and share them directly with me. This book is a response to educators' questions. I do not have all the answers, and believing so would be problematic (it would mean I am overcommitted to my thinking and unable to see multiple perspectives). I am open to investigating the questions you raise and to problem-solve them collaboratively.

Navigating this book

This book is broken into three parts:

- Part I. Foundations of SRL
- Part II. Instructional approaches for developing SRL
- Part III. Leading an SRL school improvement initiative.

The first part, Foundations of SRL, delves into the fundamental concepts and theories that underpin SRL, setting the groundwork for everything that follows. This part is designed to provide you with a deep and clear understanding of why SRL is crucial in today's educational landscape and the essential meaning of SRL. By grasping these core principles, you'll be well-equipped to explore the practical strategies, engaging activities and insightful resources outlined in Parts II and III.

At the beginning of each part – Parts I, II and III – I use the example of Alex, a middle-school teacher who is interested in SRL and is on a journey of enhancing her teaching practice to better support her young people. The short snippets of Alex at the beginning of each part offer a glimpse into the future, noting that Alex is only steps ahead of you on the journey of promoting students' SRL.

Additionally, throughout the book you will notice special sections that form the **SRL toolbox**. These are a unique feature, offering a collection of SRL strategies grounded in research to support SRL. Before you introduce these strategies to your students, you'll get the chance to experience them yourself in the context of learning about SRL. This experiential approach is crucial. It allows you to understand the activity first-hand, reap its potential benefits and build confidence in its application in your classroom. The strategies are not just theories, but practical tools that you can adapt and apply directly to your teaching environment and to your own learning.

Each chapter concludes with a chapter summary, a 'take action' section and a 'delve deeper' section. The 'take action' sections are designed to help you to start implementing SRL teaching techniques in your classroom. I encourage you to embrace a 'try it quickly' mindset with these – as soon as you read about a technique, apply it with your students and observe the immediate impact. This means you receive real-time feedback which helps you gauge what works best for your learners and context. The 'delve deeper' sections offer suggested activities to further your knowledge on each topic. These resources offer a dynamic learning experience with different modes from which to learn about SRL.

Lastly, as you know, reading is a learning experience and requires you to self-regulate as a learner. ☺ The book was designed to be read cover to cover; however, depending on your own level of knowledge about SRL, you may prefer to dip in and out of different sections – the choice is yours. Take a moment to reflect on your own goals with reading this book (e.g. what is your purpose for engaging with this book?), and the strategies you might use to help you engage with the book (e.g. using a *visual pacer* to increase focus by following the words; *annotating* connections, interesting points or important implications for your teaching; creating *reading targets*, such as reading a chapter a day or reading for 10 minutes a day). And, as is essential to SRL, continue to monitor and evaluate your reading approach, making adjustments along the way, so that you can progress your learning.

It is an absolute pleasure to be on this learning journey with you. Together, let's transform these insights into impactful practices for you and your learners.

PART I
Foundations of SRL

Alex is a middle-school teacher who is interested in helping her students self-regulate their learning more effectively.

As Alex starts to investigate her interest in SRL, she realises that SRL is not an isolated concern, but a goal documented in global and local agendas. She sees it acknowledged in multiple curricula, including the Australian Curriculum. As she keeps reading she realises that supporting her students to self-regulate their learning will require her to understand and teach a complex body of knowledge. It's more complex than she originally thought!

As Alex delves deeper into her understanding of SRL and begins to apply what she is learning to her classroom, she experiences a profound shift in the way she perceives her role as an educator and what is fundamentally important to focus on in her classroom.

In this section, we'll explore the essentials of SRL through two engaging chapters. Chapter 1 delves into why SRL is fundamentally important in the modern educational context. It provides the 'why', which is what drives Alex and can equally inspire you to integrate SRL into your teaching philosophy. Chapter 2 offers a deeper understanding of the concept of SRL. It goes beyond basic definitions to uncover the layers and nuances of SRL, mirroring Alex's learning journey.

These chapters lay the groundwork for the practical strategies and transformative insights that will follow, setting the stage for a deeper appreciation and application of SRL in your educational practice.

SRL TOOLBOX

What's your *why*?

Researchers have demonstrated that our *why* indicates the value that we place on a task (i.e. task value). The higher the value, the greater the interest, the better the performance (Edwards & Dai, 2023; Tibbetts et al., 2015).

There are three types of value beliefs (Rosenzweig et al, 2019; Wigfield and Eccles, 2020):

1. *Intrinsic value:* the task (or result of it) causes the person to experience joy.
2. *Attainment value:* the task is perceived as personally meaningful or important.
3. *Utility value:* the task is perceived as useful for current or future goals.

Research shows that when students see how their lessons connect to their personal goals and lives (i.e. attainment or utility value), they become more interested and do better in school. For instance, a study by Hulleman et al. (2010) found that college students who wrote about how their maths or psychology classes were relevant to their lives not only found the subject more interesting but also performed better academically. Similarly, Tibbetts et al. (2015) reviewed various ways to boost student motivation in school. They looked at real-life examples from high school science and college psychology classes. Their findings? When teachers help students understand the real-world value of what they're learning, students tend to become more interested and do better in their studies.

To put this into action, ask yourself:

- What's your *why* for picking up this book?
- What's your *why* for learning about SRL?
- What's your *why* for teaching SRL?

Below are a few example responses:

- 'I love learning and have a real interest in educational psychology' (intrinsic value – joy of learning).
- 'I want to be a better teacher' (attainment value – task supports future identity).
- 'I have a student who is not self-regulating their learning very well' (utility value – useful for my students).

Write your response on a post-it note and keep it close by (e.g. stick it on the front of this book, or on your laptop) so that you can constantly refer to it.

Applying the strategy in the classroom

- Start by sharing your own *why* with the class to model the process and show your own investment in the material.
- Allocate time for students to reflect on and write down their personal *whys* for SRL, the subject or specific units. Encourage them to think about intrinsic, attainment and utility value.
- Create a 'Why Wall' where students can post their *whys*, which can serve as a visual reminder of their goals and motivations.
- Regularly refer back to these *whys* in lessons to connect the material to students' personal values.

Transfer to other contexts

Consider how you might apply the 'what's your *why*?' strategy in other areas of your professional and personal life.

1
Why teach SRL?

> It's those who start with why that have the ability to inspire those around them.
>
> – Simon Sinek

For decades, researchers and entrepreneurs alike have touted the vital role of understanding the *why* behind our actions. This fundamental principle holds significant relevance in the realm of education, particularly in fostering SRL among students.

When learners recognise the reasons behind their educational pursuits this not only serves as a powerful motivational catalyst, but also aligns school goals with personal and future-focused aspirations. As teachers, without a clear comprehension of our *why* we may struggle to fully commit to teaching SRL and fail to inspire our young people to better self-regulate their learning.

In this chapter, I invite you to consider four reasons to teach SRL in schools:

- Reason 1: SRL fosters positive learning behaviours.
- Reason 2: SRL is associated with high achievement.
- Reason 3: SRL is in the curriculum.
- Reason 4: SRL is a lifelong skill set and global need.

Reason 1: SRL fosters positive learning behaviours

In my role as an education consultant and coach, educators often share with me the challenges they observe in their students' learning behaviours. In

Table 1 I document some examples of these concerns, along with a reframing of the concern as a guiding question.

Table 1. Learning behaviour concerns reframed as guiding questions

Teacher-reported concern about student learning behaviours	Reframed as a guiding question relating to SRL
Students are not adequately setting goals	How might we help students to set goals?
Students are disengaged from learning (disinterested or unmotivated)	How might we help students to better engage in their learning?
Students are not taking risks in their writing (creativity/English discipline)	How might we help students take more risks?
Students spend more time talking about performance than reflecting on the learning journey	How might we help students to focus on the learning journey rather than performance?
Some students are not speaking up in class	How might we help students to contribute during class?
New students starting at the school do not use effective note-taking strategies	How might we help students to improve their note-taking skills?
Students are distracted (not managing distractions)	How might we help students better allocate attention and achieve sustained focus for learning?
Students are not taking advantage of additional support (e.g. submitting drafts early)	How might we encourage students to leverage the support structures available to them?

All the concerns listed in Table 1 have arisen from teachers' observations of their students in classes or from their performance in subject-specific assessment tasks. While the concerns vary from motivational issues (e.g. disengaged) to help-seeking behaviours (e.g. taking advantage of support structures), the concerns all suggest that students are not self-regulating their learning very well.

Why are we concerned about these learning behaviours (or lack of)? It is because we – educators – understand (and see daily) that students who get the most out of a learning experience consistently engage in a particular set of learning behaviours: goal-setting, calculated risk-taking, help-seeking and so on. That is, they engage in SRL – and we wish that for all our students.

Reason 2: SRL is associated with high achievement

Academic achievement continues to be a cornerstone of a student's educational journey and a critical metric for assessing school efficacy. It is more than just a measure of learning; it represents a student's ability to grasp, apply and integrate knowledge across various disciplines. High academic achievement opens doors to advanced education opportunities and better career prospects. It is positively correlated with a range of beneficial life outcomes, including higher self-esteem and overall wellbeing.

Those who effectively manage their learning processes, set goals and monitor their progress often display higher levels of academic success. Indeed, multiple studies have demonstrated a strong correlation between SRL and attainment (Muijs & Bokhove, 2020; Elhusseini et al., 2022).

The correlation between SRL and academic achievement is particularly evident in the context of blended learning (i.e. a combination of face-to-face and online learning experiences), an approach that is becoming more common in schools. Self-regulation is key to achievement in a blended learning context due to the reduced direct supervision and structured learning environments found in traditional classroom settings. Xu et al. (2023) examined an impressive array of 163 studies from various countries (albeit in higher education). The results aligned with previous findings, highlighting that SRL strategies are not just beneficial but perhaps essential for academic success in modern learning contexts.

Reason 3: SRL is in the curriculum

SRL is documented in different curricula across the world. For example, the International Baccalaureate (IB) program, a globally recognised educational curriculum, places a significant emphasis on SRL. This emphasis is most clearly reflected in the IB Learner Profile, a set of ten attributes that describe the qualities an IB education aspires to develop in students. For example, being 'Knowledgeable' and 'Reflective' aligns with an SRL focus, as students are encouraged to not only acquire in-depth knowledge but also to reflect on their learning processes and outcomes. The 'Reflective' attribute, in particular, is a cornerstone of SRL, as it involves students actively evaluating their strengths and weaknesses, setting learning goals and adjusting their strategies accordingly.

Additionally, the Council of the European Union (2018, Article 7) stated their focus regarding the key competencies for lifelong learning:

Skills, such as problem solving, critical thinking, ability to cooperate, creativity, computational thinking, self-regulation are more essential than ever before in our quickly changing society. They are the tools to make what has been learned work in real time, in order to generate new ideas, new theories, new products, and new knowledge.

The Netherlands' curriculum reform also emphasises SRL, and this is evident in the Organisation for Economic Cooperation and Development's (OECD, 2019a) *Education 2030 Curriculum Content Mapping: An Analysis of the Netherlands curriculum proposal*. The proposal documents that the curriculum reform aims to foster students' abilities to independently manage their learning processes, enabling them to adapt to and navigate the complexities of a rapidly evolving world. This comprises key skills and attributes that integrate key aspects of metacognition, self-regulation and learning to learn. This approach aligns with the broader objectives of preparing students for future challenges and reflects a commitment to equipping students with the skills necessary for lifelong learning and adaptation.

Here in Australia, increased attention has been directed towards the skill set of SRL, acknowledging it as essential for lifelong learning, enabling learners to be capable of and committed to a process of ongoing upskilling and retraining (Council of Australian Governments Education Council, 2019). Australian state and territory governments are documenting SRL as a subgoal under broader goals directed towards lifelong learning. For example, *The Future of Education: An ACT education strategy for the next ten years* (ACT Education Directorate, 2018) outlines four foundations for education improvement efforts, the first being positioning students at the centre of learning, further detailing that all students are active learners who demonstrate self-control as they successfully navigate their learning journey – in other words, they are self-regulated learners.

The Australian Curriculum, Assessment and Reporting Authority (ACARA, 2024) has integrated a focus on SRL within more than one category of the general capabilities. For example, the personal and social capability indicates a focus on developing self-awareness and self-management, which are two key components of SRL. Additionally, the critical and creative thinking capability highlights a need for students to be engaged in high-quality metacognition, which is a fundamental component of SRL; see Table 2.

Table 2. Elements of the Australian Curriculum V9 General Capabilities that relate to SRL

		Sub-Elements of the General Capabilities related to SRL
Personal and Social Capability	Self-awareness	**Personal awareness** – students develop an appreciation of their personal qualities and areas for growth. Through acknowledgement and assessment of their thoughts, feelings, actions and abilities, students can plan for growth across a range of contexts.
		Emotional awareness – students explore the factors that influence emotions in themselves and in others, and how emotional responses affect behaviour in a range of contexts.
		Reflective practice – students reflect cyclically on feedback and self-assessment to evaluate their learning and the factors, personal or otherwise, that influence this learning.
	Self-management	**Goal-setting** – students develop the organisational and planning behaviours needed to set, adapt and achieve goals.
		Emotional regulation – students constructively express, manage, monitor and evaluate their emotional responses in a range of contexts.
		Perseverance and adaptability – students persist in the face of setbacks and frustrations. They learn to review and modify their approaches when faced with challenges and to build strategies to complete tasks and overcome obstacles.
Critical and Creative Thinking	Reflecting	**Think about thinking (metacognition)** – students identify, describe and evaluate the thinking and learning strategies that they use to complete activities. They reflect on the ways that their thinking, and the approaches they take, may be influenced by external contributions or viewpoints.
		Transfer knowledge – students make connections between their current knowledge and skills, and new contexts where they can adapt and use what they already know and can do. Both critical and creative thinking are involved, and new contexts can include other learning areas of the curriculum.

ADAPTED FROM ACARA (2024).

Gonski et al. (2018) recommended that the Australian Government 'give more prominence to the acquisition of the general capabilities e.g., critical and creative thinking, personal and social capability' (p. xii), essentially advising that teachers adopt a greater focus on the development of students' SRL skills. Additionally, the Council of Australian Governments Education Council (2019) endorsed the Alice Springs (Mparntwe) Declaration, the united vision for a world class education system for young people in Australia, which documented the goal that 'all young Australians become… successful lifelong learners' (p. 4) and detailed this goal with a number of explicit statements related to SRL (e.g. 'develop their ability and motivation to learn and play an active role in their own learning'; 'are responsive and adaptive to new ways of thinking and learning', p. 7).

Reason 4: SRL is a lifelong skill set and global need

All these policies and different curricula point to a shared understanding that SRL is a vital skill set for lifelong learning, and a highly sought-after skill set in the workforce. The value of this skill set is emphasised as the current job landscape changes with the acceleration of technology, particularly the advent of AI, and the shift towards online educational resources. As already mentioned, roles requiring repetitive tasks are being automated, underscoring the importance of continuous learning and adaptation for both the current workforce and students who represent the future workforce. Globalisation has further complicated the landscape by allowing rapid information exchange across borders. This change requires significant reforms in the systems that support learners to self-regulate when engaging with such large volumes of information.

Additionally, in the OECD's Learning Compass 2030 (OECD 2019b), SRL and metacognition are recognised as essential components of the skills necessary for future success. This framework, developed as part of the OECD Future of Education and Skills 2030 project, highlights the importance of cognitive and metacognitive skills, which encompass critical thinking, creative thinking, learning to learn, and self-regulation. These skills are seen as key to students effectively using their knowledge and abilities to meet complex demands and achieve their goals.

Chapter summary

In this chapter we explored the contemporary importance of SRL in educational settings. We considered four key reasons why we must prioritise teaching SRL: to address our concerns as educators, the correlation between

SRL and high academic achievement, its inclusion in different curricula internationally and here in Australia, and the important role of SRL in nurturing lifelong learning. In essence, SRL is more than a curriculum necessity; it is an essential skill for students' overall development. This highlights the value of understanding and implementing SRL teaching approaches in classrooms and schools. Were the reasons we explored similar or different to your response to the 'What's my why?' strategy? By offering you four reasons, I hoped to strengthen your value belief (your why) for teaching SRL. As previously mentioned, the higher the value, the greater the interest, the better the performance.

Take action

Help students understand the *why* of SRL by sharing with them reasons why they should want to become self-regulated learners (e.g. skill set as a lifelong learner; associated with high achievement).

Delve deeper

My website **shyambarr.com/book** includes links to the following resources so you can explore the concepts in this chapter further.

- ☐ View the Australian Curriculum (V9), and consider the personal and social capability, or the critical and creative thinking capability.
- ☐ Read Vosniadou et al (2021) 'Teaching students how to learn: Setting the stage for lifelong learning'. Start with the section titled 'Developing the capability necessary for lifelong learning is important for success in school and life in the twenty first century', pages 18–21.
- ☐ Read the OECD's (2019) Future of Education and Skills 2030 – Conceptual Learning Framework – Learning Compass 2030, particularly pages 5–10: 'Cognitive skills are essential; metacognitive skills are becoming so'.

SRL TOOLBOX

What's the cost of *not* taking action?

In the previous SRL toolkit section we discussed task value and its role in generating motivation. We often consider the costs of taking action or engaging in an activity (Tibbetts et al., 2015; Bruning et al., 2010) – for example, the costs associated with teaching SRL might be time, workload and attention. When the costs seem to outweigh the value of the activity, we might not be motivated to take action. However, we can flip the concept to consider the costs of *not* taking action to instigate a higher level of task value and therefore motivation.

Take a moment to respond to the following questions:

- What is the cost of *not* taking action (i.e. *not* teaching SRL)?
- What might happen if we *don't* act now (i.e. if we *don't* teach SRL)?

Applying the strategy in the classroom

You can teach your students to ask themselves the motivational question: 'what's the cost of *not* taking action?'.

For example, in the context of students self-regulating their learning, you could say:

> *A strategy that I use when I want to increase my motivation is asking myself, 'what's the cost of not taking action?'. In other words, what might happen if I didn't act now – if I didn't improve the way I self-regulate my learning? Poor performance? Not achieving my goals? Not setting myself up for success in the future?'*

Ask students to share the consequences or costs of not taking action with their SRL with the class.

Let's look at another example, in the context of taking risks in creative writing. You could say:

> *A strategy that I use when I want to increase my motivation is asking myself, 'what's the cost of not taking action?'. In other words, what might happen if I didn't act now – if I didn't take a risk with my vocabulary or other elements of creative writing?*

A simple way to test the effect of the strategy is to run a simple pre-post assessment of students' motivation for the task. For example, say to students: 'On a scale of 1–10 (1 being low motivation, 10 being high motivation) how motivated are you to take risks in this creative writing piece?' Then, after explicitly teaching them the 'what's the cost of *not* taking action' strategy and getting them to respond to the question, ask them to re-evaluate their motivation on a scale of 1–10. Was there a change in the score? If yes, could this change be attributed to the strategy? Providing immediate evidence to students will help them see the value in applying a strategy, and a simple pre-post assessment can generate some simple, yet immediate, evidence.

Transfer to other contexts

In what ways can this strategy be applied to different subjects or courses you learn or teach?

Activate prior knowledge

Activating prior knowledge is a cognitive strategy that helps you comprehend new information because you can relate the new information to your existing knowledge. Hattan et al. (2023) conducted a systematic literature review of 54 articles, exploring the specific techniques and optimal conditions for activating prior knowledge to enhance learners' comprehension. They identified a range of activation strategies, including open-ended prompts (e.g. 'Generate any ideas that come to mind when thinking about SRL') and visual representations (e.g. concept maps). They reported that prompting learners to activate their knowledge was extremely beneficial at different points throughout a reading experience.

To activate your own prior knowledge about SRL, you can:

- Generate any ideas that come to mind when you think of the term 'SRL'.
- Describe SRL in your own words.

Alternatively, you can use the Generate-Sort-Connect-Elaborate thinking routine (adapted from Ritchart et al., 2011) to develop a concept map of ideas about SRL:

- *Generate* a list of ideas and initial thoughts that come to mind when you think about SRL.
- *Sort* your ideas according to how central or tangential they are. Place central ideas near the middle and more tangential ideas towards the outside of the page.
- *Connect* your ideas by drawing lines between ideas that have something in common. Label each connection in your network, explaining how the two ideas are connected.
- *Elaborate* on any of the ideas/thoughts you have written so far by adding new ideas that expand, extend or add to them.

Applying the strategy in the classroom

Consider asking students what they know about SRL or facilitating the Generate-Sort-Connect-Elaborate strategy with your students.

Transfer to other contexts

Students can activate their prior knowledge about SRL in different subject contexts, or activate their prior knowledge about a subject-specific topic before learning about that topic. The key here is that the learner is selecting an 'activating prior knowledge' strategy because they understand the benefits of this strategy for learning.

2
What is SRL, really?

> If you change the way you look at things,
> the things you look at change.
>
> — Wayne Dyer

SRL is a complex concept. It's a metaphorical elephant; and as Desmond Tutu famously said, 'There is only one way to eat an elephant: a bite at a time'.

In this chapter I'll break the concept of SRL into seven components to aid our understanding of what it really is and what it is not.

SRL is different to self-directed learning

As mentioned earlier in this book, SRL can be defined as:

> *the capability to understand your own thinking, motivations, emotions and behaviours in the context of learning, and to monitor and change these in response to a problem or towards a desired goal.*

SRL shares similarities with other common educational terms such as 'self-management', 'metacognition' and 'metalearning'. However, it is often confused with 'self-directed learning'. To help clear up any confusion, I have documented some of the differences between these two approaches in Table 3.

Table 3 highlights that SRL is required in self-directed learning tasks that are autonomously led by students, but also in tasks designed and facilitated by the teacher. In other words: successful self-directed learning requires SRL; but successful SRL does not require self-directed learning.

Table 3. Differences between SRL and self-directed learning

Self-regulated learning (SRL)	Self-directed learning
Emphasises metacognitive, motivational, behavioural and social aspects. SRL is about understanding your own cognition in the social environment, and effectively using this awareness to regulate learning.	**Emphasises autonomy and independence in learning.** Self-directed learning is driven by the learner's desire to learn.
Focuses on how learners manage their learning process. SRL involves setting goals, monitoring progress and adjusting strategies to achieve academic objectives.	**Focuses on learners taking the initiative in their learning.** Self-directed learning involves learners making decisions about their learning goals, resources and evaluation of learning outcomes.
Often occurs within structured learning environments and geared towards achieving specific educational outcomes. SRL strategies are applied in settings with specific learning objectives, such as classrooms, and are closely aligned with curricular goals and academic standards.	**More common in informal or unstructured settings.** Self-directed learning is prevalent in adult learning, professional development and personal interest areas.
Teacher-guided in a formal education setting. Teachers play a significant role in developing SRL skills among students.	**Learner-driven with minimal instructor involvement.** The learner is the primary decision-maker in self-directed learning, often without direct teacher guidance.

SRL is an umbrella term

SRL is considered a broad 'umbrella' term (Panadero, 2017) as it consists of multiple variables that influence learning – refer Figure 2.

Many researchers have acknowledged three main knowledge categories of SRL:

1. **metacognition:** how a learner thinks about and regulates their cognition
2. **cognition:** how a learner thinks
3. **motivation:** a learner's reason to act.

Dr Patrick Sins, Professor of Learning at Rotterdam University of Applied Sciences (Netherlands), shared the following metaphor with me:

> *SRL is a toolbox containing three tools: cognitive strategies (the 'processors' with which you interpret and internalise knowledge), metacognitive strategies (the 'managers' who tell you which method to use) and motivational strategies (the 'motors' that drive you).*

Some researchers have extended SRL to include **resource management**: how a learner manages the resources within their environment, such as seeking help from a teacher, knowing who might help, and engaging in discussion and critique with other students (e.g. Lee et al., 2023; Perry et al., 2020). A few others have explicitly acknowledged **emotion**: how emotions influence a learning experience (e.g. Vosniadou et al., 2021). The five categories listed within Figure 2 fundamentally underpin SRL because they encompass the entirety of the learning process, from the internal motivations and thought processes that initiate learning to the external resources and emotional context that sustain it. Together, they form a comprehensive framework that addresses not only the acquisition of knowledge but also the self-awareness and environmental interaction necessary for learners to adapt and apply their learning effectively.

Figure 2. SRL as an umbrella term

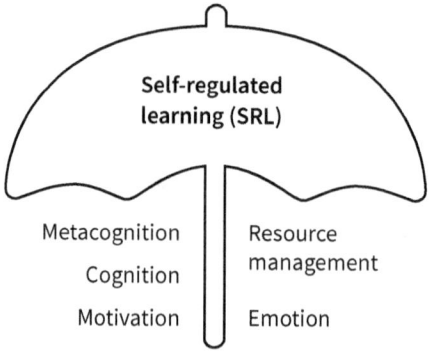

To better encompass the complex body of knowledge that underpins SRL, I have expanded these five categories to acknowledge the many subcategories they cover. My SRL knowledge framework is not an exhaustive list, but a constantly evolving framework as I delve deeper into the field of SRL. My expanded set of the five categories can be seen as a visual display in Figure 3 with brief descriptions of the categories and subcategories of SRL documented in Table 4.

In Figure 3, **metacognition** is positioned at the top to acknowledge its fundamental role in the process of SRL, as discussed in detail later in this chapter. The other categories of motivation, cognition, resource management and emotion are listed below as they are each complex bodies of knowledge in their own right, but require metacognition to act upon in the process of planning, monitoring and evaluating your learning. Although I have separated the categories with the intention of helping you grapple with the framework, the categories do not exist in isolation and are constantly interacting with the other categories, a learner's behaviour and their environment.

Motivation refers to the learner's reason to act (or not act). Self-regulated learners are typically intrinsically motivated to learn; however, they recognise the constant variation in their motivation for different learning tasks. They understand the different motivational beliefs that influence their motivation for learning and can enact different strategies to help them act for learning, especially when their motivation may initially be lacking. As a result, they are better prepared to persevere towards their long-term goals in the face of challenge, failure or an unexpected result.

Cognition includes a range of cognitive functions such as how learners process information, allocate attention, manage their cognitive load and navigate the brain's cognitive biases. A self-regulated learner understands and is aware of these cognitive processes and possesses strategies to help them better encode and retrieve information for long-term recall and application. This includes being able to effectively allocate their attention to focus and achieve flow in a task (Csikszentmihalyi, 2009). These learners see value in activating prior knowledge and have access to a suite of tools to help them engage in deep encoding and transfer.

Resource management refers to how learners restructure their environments to achieve optimal learning. Self-regulated learners understand the importance of changing location, moving away from peers and/or isolating technology that may not support their immediate learning. They are effective time managers and have wellconsidered strategies to help them prioritise tasks and allocate time in a schedule. They have effective organisational systems across physical and digital resources (utilising folders or online systems to organise and store knowledge). Self-regulated learners also understand how well they have progressed and have avenues to seek help; they know, for example, when to consult a textbook, speak to or collaborate with a peer, and/or engage with an online support tool or teacher.

For students to self-regulate their learning they must have an awareness and control of **emotion**. Self-regulated learners recognise stress when it is emerging and know how to manage task and performance anxiety to minimise negative impacts on learning. They understand the relationship between their emotional state and the quality of their engagement in learning, actively seeking to maintain a positive sense of wellbeing. Self-regulated learners have a range of strategies to help them navigate their emotional states, such as journalling, mindfulness and box breathing.

Figure 3. SRL knowledge framework

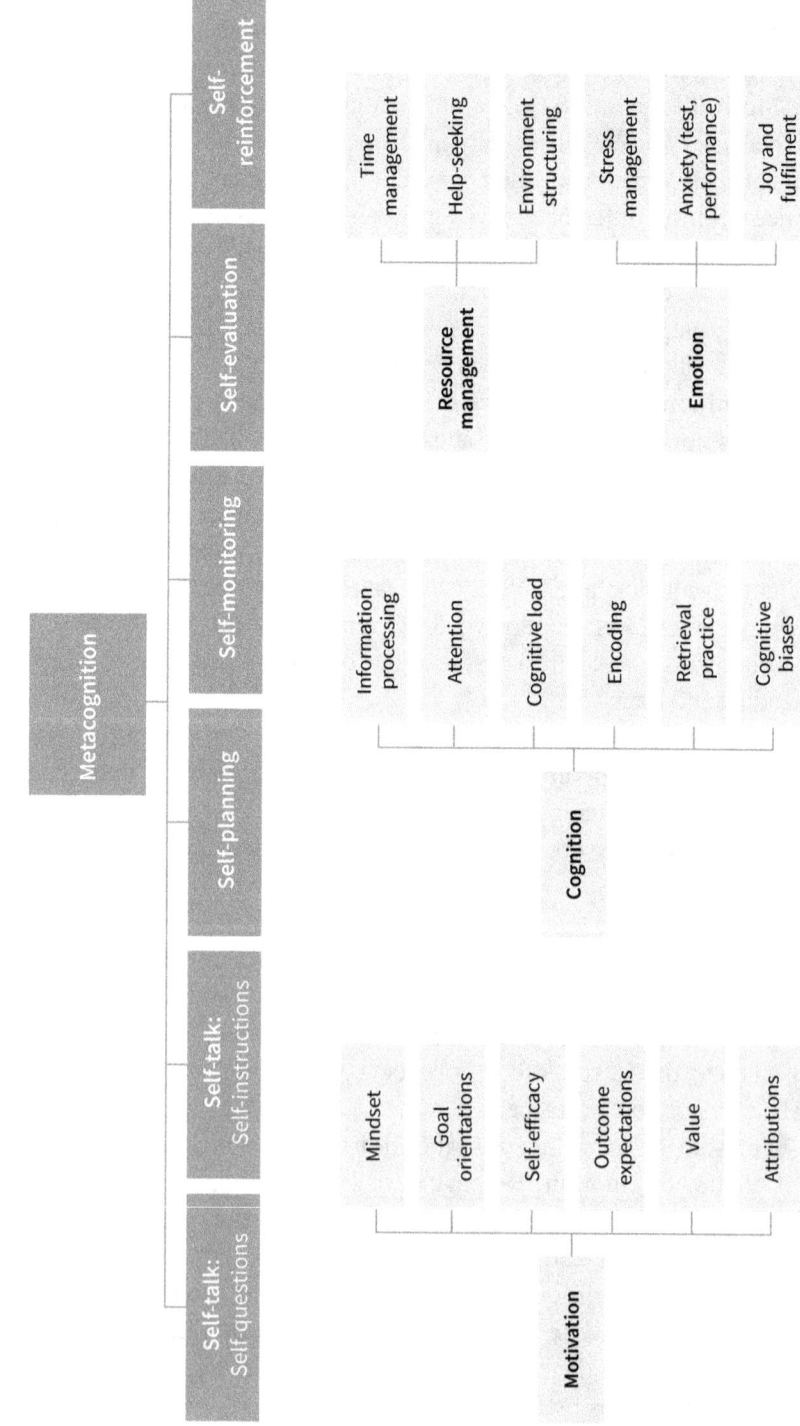

30 Educate to Self-Regulate

Table 4. SRL knowledge framework categories and subcategories

Main category	Subcategory	Description
Metacognition	Self-talk: Self-questions	Reflecting on your own understanding and knowledge by asking yourself a question.
	Self-talk: Self-instructions	Guiding yourself through tasks or problems.
	Self-planning	Strategising on approaches for tasks or learning.
	Self-monitoring	Checking your own progress towards a goal.
	Self-evaluation	Assessing your own performance or understanding.
	Self-reinforcement	Rewarding yourself for meeting goals or performing well.
Motivation	Mindset	Your belief about whether your intelligence is fixed or malleable.
	Goal orientations	The personal goals set that direct behaviour.
	Self-efficacy	Belief in your own ability to succeed in specific situations or accomplish tasks.
	Outcome expectations	Anticipations about the consequences of actions.
	Value	The importance you place on various aspects of learning.
	Attributions	How you explain the causes of your own and others' actions and outcomes.
Cognition	Information processing	The way in which information is encoded, stored and retrieved in and from memory.
	Attention	The concentration and focus on tasks or information.
	Cognitive load	The total amount of mental effort being used in the working memory.
	Encoding	The process of converting information into a form that can be stored in memory.
	Retrieval practice	The act of recalling information from memory with little or no cues.
	Cognitive biases	Systematic patterns of deviation from norm or rationality in judgement.

Main category	Subcategory	Description
Resource management	Time management	Organising and planning how to divide time between specific activities.
	Help-seeking	The process of finding and soliciting support as needed.
	Environment structuring	Organising your physical and digital space to enhance learning.
Emotion	Stress management	Techniques aimed at controlling your level of stress.
	Anxiety (test, performance)	Nervousness or worry about an impending task or performance.
	Joy and fulfilment	The feeling of great pleasure and happiness.

SRL requires metacognition

For a learner to activate their SRL knowledge and skills (the umbrella) during learning requires the higher-order cognitive process of metacognition. **Metacognition** is often defined as 'thinking about thinking'. However, 'thinking about thinking' or having *knowledge* of our thinking (i.e. cognition) is only the first of two layers of metacognition (Brown et al., 1981). The second layer is regulation of our thinking, having strategies to monitor and *control* thinking (i.e. self-regulation). Refer Figure 4.

Figure 4. Layers of thinking

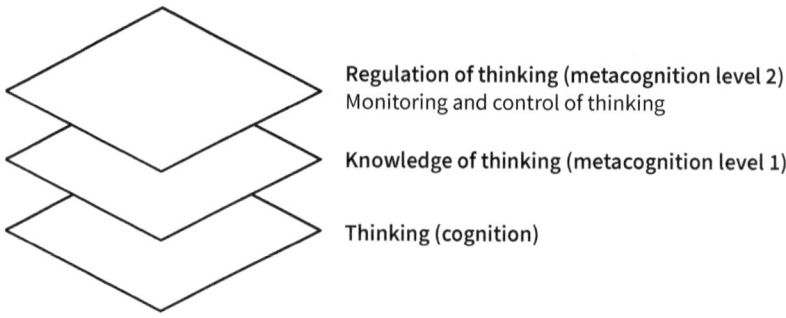

Starting at the bottom of Figure 4, the first layer is cognition – **thinking**. The second and third layers are metacognition, including **knowledge of**

thinking and **regulation of thinking**. **Knowledge of thinking** incorporates learners' understanding of their thinking processes, such as how they process information and store it in different memory systems. With knowledge of thinking as a foundation, **regulation of thinking** can now occur. To regulate thinking the learner must first *monitor their thinking* by asking questions such as, 'Does this make sense? Do I comprehend the task? Is my response sufficient? Will I remember the essential information?'. Depending on the learner's reflection during their monitoring, they may then need to *control their thinking* by, for example, choosing to dedicate more time to study, changing their method of revision or seeking help from alternative sources (Roebers, 2017).

Let's revisit the 'living room of the mind' metaphor that I shared at the start of this book. This metaphor directly acknowledges each level of metacognition; refer Figure 5.

Figure 5. The living room of the mind and metacognition

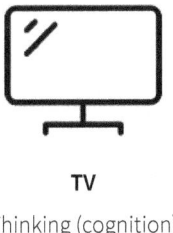  

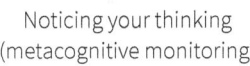

TV	Sitting on the couch watching the TV	Using the remote to change the channel on the TV
Thinking (cognition)	Noticing your thinking (metacognitive monitoring)	Self-regulation (metacognitive control)

The 'living room of the mind' metaphor is a more accessible way to explain the different levels of metacognition and SRL to students.

One of my pre-service teachers, Brad Milosevic, liked the idea of the remote so much that he drafted an exemplar that he could model with his students as he invited them to draw up their own 'SRL remotes' – refer Figure 6, overleaf.

Figure 6. Example of SRL remote

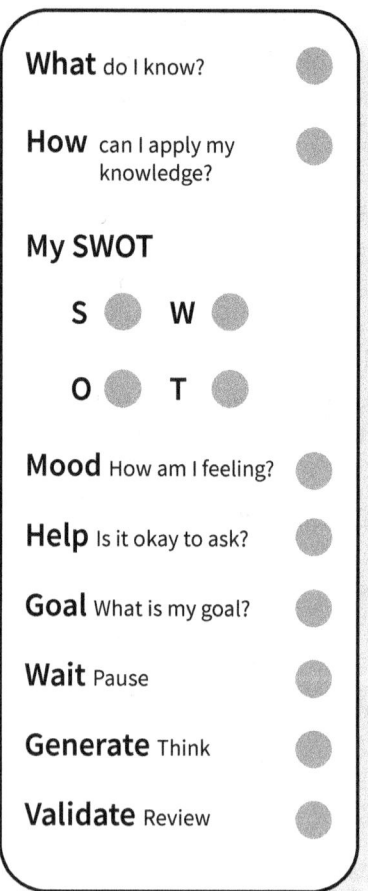

SOURCE: BRAD MILOSEVIC

There are many different strategies (buttons) that might exist on a learner's SRL remote; I've included some examples in Table 5.

Table 5 demonstrates the vast body of strategic knowledge that a student can draw on as they self-regulate their learning. The quality of this knowledge of themselves as learners, their learning processes and the strategies they use to regulate their learning will influence the extent to which they are able to self-regulate their learning at any given point during the day.

Table 5. Examples of SRL strategies

Strategy category	Description	Common examples
Metacognitive learning strategies	Strategies that support engagement in planning, monitoring and evaluating learning	• Goal-setting strategies (e.g. SMART goals) • Self-questions to support comprehension monitoring (e.g. 'Do I understand this?') • Self-assessment and self-evaluation strategies (e.g. how to use a rubric or learning continuum to plan or evaluate learning; self-testing)
Cognitive learning strategies	Strategies that are used to process and remember information	• Activating prior knowledge • Text comprehension strategies (e.g. annotating, underlining) • Note-taking strategies (e.g. summarising) • Concept mapping • Flash cards • Retrieval practice • Distributed practice • Rereading • Highlighting and annotating
Motivational learning strategies	Strategies that are applied to support attention and focus, along with initiation and perseverance with a task	• Understanding why a task is worth doing • Self-rewarding • Doing the most fun task first • Growth mindset strategies (e.g. adding *yet* to absolute statements)
Resource management strategies	Strategies that manipulate the environment to support learning	• Time-management strategies • Help-seeking strategies • Setting up a suitable study environment
Emotional regulation strategies	Strategies that support positive emotions for learning and minimise emotions that negatively influence learning processes	• Meditation/mindfulness • Breathing techniques • Stress reduction techniques • Gratitude practice

ADAPTED FROM DE SMUL ET AL. (2018) AND BARR (2021).

SRL is an active process

To engage in SRL, a learner must metacognitively activate their SRL knowledge as they engage in three phases of SRL: planning, monitoring and evaluating. Refer Figure 7.

Figure 7. The three phases of SRL

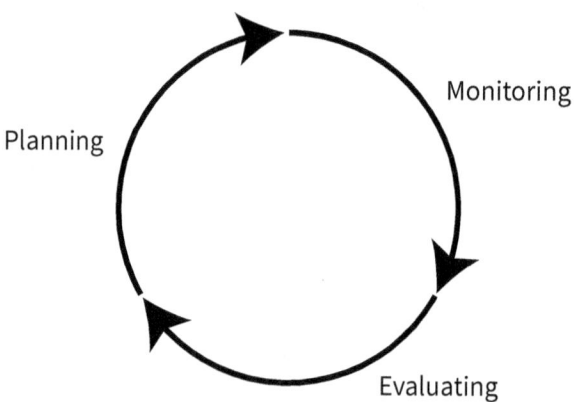

ADAPTED FROM PINTRICH (1999) AND ZIMMERMAN (2011).

SRL is not a linear process; however, in Figure 7 the three phases are documented as a cycle for ease of understanding. I will explain the process of SRL by starting at the planning phase and progressing through to the monitoring and evaluating phases.

Planning phase

In the planning phase, a learner might use metacognitive strategies to assess the task at hand and set appropriate goals. For example, they could use self-talk to question their understanding of the subject ('What do I know about this topic?') and give themselves instructions ('First, I'll outline the main concepts'). They might use planning to break down the task into manageable parts and decide on the resources they need, such as textbooks or study groups.

They would apply knowledge of their mindset to approach the task with a growth mindset, believing that their abilities can be developed through hard work, which increases motivation. They would consider their goal orientations (e.g. mastery versus performance goals) to ensure they are aiming to understand the material deeply rather than just aiming for a good grade. They might also reflect on value to connect the task to their personal or career goals, which can increase their intrinsic motivation to learn.

Monitoring phase

During the monitoring phase, the learner engages in self-monitoring to keep track of their progress and cognitive load to ensure they are not overwhelmed. They might use attention management strategies to stay focused and regularly check if their study techniques are working well. The learner would also draw upon resource management skills such as time management to allocate sufficient time for each part of the task, and environment structuring to create a distraction-free study environment.

Evaluating phase

In the evaluating phase, the learner would engage in self-evaluation to compare their performance against their goals. They might reflect on the attribution of their success or failure, whether it was due to internal factors such as effort or external factors such as task difficulty. Emotion also plays a role; the learner needs to manage stress and anxiety, especially if the outcomes are not as expected, and seek joy and fulfilment from the learning process, which can reinforce motivation for future learning tasks. Additionally, self-reinforcement might be used to reward themselves for achieving goals, which can be as simple as taking a break or treating themselves to something enjoyable after a long study session.

In summary, a learner engaged in SRL uses a variety of cognitive, metacognitive, motivational and emotional strategies to plan, monitor and evaluate their learning. They are proactive in seeking out and using these strategies to optimise their learning process and outcomes.

SRL is a decision-making process and a daily practice

The moment of 'metacognitive regulation' in SRL involves a learner choosing to stop one thing and do another – they have to make decisions. Therefore, SRL is a decision-making process. For example, if a learner becomes aware that their note-taking approach is ineffective, they may choose to stop that approach and adopt a new, more effective study technique.

A learner's ability to make productive decisions for learning is influenced by various internal and external factors, such as sleep, nutrition, cognitive biases and decision fatigue – the idea that as your decisions compound over the day, your ability to make certain decisions wanes and can result in you opting for safe options over risk-taking (Danziger et al., 2011). This dependent relationship between SRL and decision-making capability means that SRL is, in essence, a daily practice. In other words, while we aim to support our students' development of SRL knowledge, we recognise that even the most knowledgeable self-regulated learner may not self-regulate their learning in some instances. When we acknowledge SRL as a decision-making process and a daily practice, we shift from seeking perfection in students' SRL performance, to seeking levels of consistency in their SRL performance as an indicator of their SRL capabilities.

SRL is influenced by the environment

In exploring the intricacies of SRL within the framework of Bandura's (2001) model of reciprocal determinism, it becomes imperative to delve into the core principle of this theory. Reciprocal determinism, as posited by Bandura, suggests that human behaviour is a product of the interplay among personal factors, behavioural patterns, and environmental influences. This triadic reciprocality means that our actions are not solely the result of internal dispositions or external conditions, but rather a continuous interaction between the two, along with the behaviours we exhibit.

When situating SRL within the model of reciprocal determinism, it becomes apparent that SRL transcends merely being a manifestation of one's personal (cognitive, affective and motivational) and behavioural factors. SRL is intricately linked to the environment in which an individual operates, underpinning the notion that learning is neither solely autonomous nor entirely dictated by external forces. This viewpoint aligns with the understanding that SRL is a dynamic process, where learners continuously interact with their environment, adapting their strategies and behaviours in response to the changing context. The co-regulatory aspect of SRL emphasises that while individuals actively regulate their learning processes, this self-regulation is invariably influenced and shaped by the social context and interactions with others. Hence, SRL can be viewed as being co-constructed within the social environment, highlighting the significance of social interactions in the development and execution of self-regulatory practices.

Nevertheless, the assertion that SRL is always a co-regulatory process within the social environment warrants careful consideration. While the social context undeniably plays a critical role in shaping self-regulatory behaviours, it is also essential to recognise the capacity of individuals to exert personal agency over their learning processes. The extent to which SRL is influenced by social co-regulation may vary depending on the individual's level of self-efficacy, the task at hand and the specific environmental conditions. Therefore, while it is valid to argue that SRL is often co-constructed with others in the social environment, acknowledging the nuances and variations in how individuals engage with and are influenced by their surroundings is crucial. This balanced perspective allows for a deeper understanding of SRL within the model of reciprocal determinism, recognising the interplay between personal agency and social influences in the self-regulation of learning.

SRL is both domain-specific and general

Many argue that SRL is domain-specific, meaning that the strategies and cognitive processes students employ to regulate their learning are uniquely tailored to the particular subject matter or context at hand. This concept emphasises that the effectiveness of SRL strategies is not universally transferable across different subjects, but rather is deeply entrenched within the specific demands and nature of each educational domain.

For instance, the strategies a student uses in a mathematics class, which might emphasise problem-solving and logical reasoning, can differ significantly from those used in a literature class, where analytical and interpretative skills are more prominently required. This reflects the inherent differences in the nature of knowledge and skills between domains, which necessitates different SRL strategies. In mathematics, SRL might involve setting specific procedural steps to solve an equation, whereas in literature, it might involve drafting and revising a critical analysis.

An alternative view (and where I side) is that a learning activity involves a combination of domain-specific SRL strategies and more general SRL strategies. For example, during a learning activity, a student is likely to engage a general SRL strategy, such as a goal-setting strategy (a metacognitive planning strategy), and combine it with domain-specific strategies such as the application of a particular algebraic formula. Similarly, the student might self-evaluate (general metacognitive strategy) the application and effectiveness of the algebraic formula (domain-specific strategy).

Other factors that influence SRL

In this section, I briefly discuss other factors that influence SRL, including gender, socio-economic background, age and development, and learning difficulties. For a more comprehensive analysis, refer to Muijs and Bokhove's (2020) review.

Gender and socio-economic background

According to Veenman et al. (2006), the development of SRL skills is partially dependent on the opportunities provided in the home environment, which often correlate with social background. This implies that students from more privileged backgrounds may have better opportunities to develop these skills. Leutwyler and Maag Merki (2009) supported this by pointing out that the acquisition and application of metacognition, a key component of SRL, is influenced by gender and socio-economic background, favouring females and students from high socio-economic backgrounds.

Interestingly, studies repeatedly show girls outperforming boys in SRL across different phases of schooling (see Muijs & Bokhove, 2020, for review). Despite these differences, the structure of relationships between metacognitive skills and factors such as attainment or goal mastery does not appear to differ significantly between genders.

The impact of socio-economic status (SES) on SRL and metacognition presents a more complex picture. While there is a modest correlation between higher SES and the use of metacognitive strategies, the relationship is not straightforward. Interventions have shown improvements in metacognitive skills and attainment among low SES students, but these do not consistently surpass the performance of their higher SES peers (Muijs & Bokhove, 2020). This indicates that while SRL and metacognitive training can benefit students from disadvantaged backgrounds, they may not necessarily bridge the attainment gap between different SES groups without other appropriate support and intervention.

Age and development

One of the most common questions that I am asked in workshops is, 'Are my students old enough to engage in SRL?' You might be thinking your students are too young to be able to self-regulate their learning.

Aspects of SRL have been observed in children as young as three years old. Whitebread et al. (2009) argued that children under six years of age possess metacognitive skills, but these are difficult to illuminate due to their developing verbal skills (i.e. they have difficulty thinking-aloud). For example, when presented with age-appropriate and meaningful tasks, young children's behaviours suggest strategic thinking (thinking about strategies and an approach to achieve a goal, predicting and self-evaluating performance). Bernard et al. (2015) reported that children as young as three years old opt out of activities depending on the perceived level of difficulty, indicating that young learners self-judge their level of comfort with a task and choose whether to participate or not.

Muijs and Bokhove (2020, p. 14) summarised the developmental trajectory as follows:

- By the age of approximately three:
  - Children begin to possess an understanding of their own cognitive processes.
  - They can differentiate thinking about something from the direct experience of seeing it.
  - The word 'think' enters their vocabulary.
- Approaching age four:
  - Children start to grasp that other people have their own thoughts and beliefs.
  - They come to realize that these thoughts and beliefs can be different from their own perspectives.
- As children move from five to eight years old:
  - The early stages of awareness about memory processes and cognitive understanding start to appear.
- From ages eight to ten:
  - The development of skills for thinking about one's own thinking processes begins to take shape.

Learning difficulties

Students with learning difficulties often face challenges in SRL due to deficits in executive functions, which are critical for planning, monitoring and evaluating their learning processes (Desoete & Roeyers, 2005; King & McInerney, 2016). These students may struggle with setting realistic goals, employing effective strategies and assessing their own understanding and performance. Targeted interventions that scaffold and explicitly teach SRL strategies can be beneficial to support them. These interventions can help students with learning difficulties to become more aware of their cognitive processes, regulate their motivational beliefs and employ adaptive emotional strategies, leading to improved academic outcomes (Donker et al., 2014).

Beliefs that get in the way of teaching SRL

At this point, you might find yourself asking:

- Can SRL really be taught or is it something that naturally develops with time?
- Are my students capable of SRL? At what age can I expect students to start self-regulating their learning?
- Is it my responsibility to teach students how to self-regulate their learning?
- How do I help my students self-regulate their learning when I'm not great at self-regulating myself?

While all these questions are worthwhile exploring, they may indicate some subconscious beliefs about learning that could enable or hinder your efforts in promoting students' SRL. In Table 6 I give some examples of limiting and enabling beliefs in relation to SRL.

Table 6. Limiting versus enabling beliefs about SRL

Limiting belief	Enabling belief
Knowledge about SRL is acquired implicitly through experience and does not need to be explicitly taught.	SRL can be explicitly taught.
SRL is different in character compared to other curriculum content knowledge.	SRL is a complex body of knowledge.
Knowledge about learning and SRL is not used all that often.	SRL knowledge accompanies task knowledge.
The most important knowledge about SRL is practical rather than theoretical.	A theoretical understanding supports practical knowledge.
I do not know how to effectively teach SRL (I lack confidence in my ability to teach SRL).	High self-efficacy is required to effectively teach SRL.
SRL is primarily the responsibility of the student, not the teacher.	The teacher influences SRL in a classroom, so also shares responsibility.
SRL strategies are relevant only for specific groups within the student population.	All students can benefit from developing SRL strategies and engaging in deliberate practice in different contexts.

Limiting belief	Enabling belief
SRL is inherently unteachable, and therefore it need not be the subject of explicit instruction.	SRL can be explicitly taught.
I have too many other competing priorities to teach SRL.	SRL is a core lifelong learning skill and is arguably a critical priority in schools.
My students aren't capable of SRL.	SRL capabilities have been observed in children as young as three years old.

ADAPTED FROM LAWSON ET AL. (2018).

The beliefs documented in Table 6 highlight various perspectives that can shape how teachers approach the teaching of SRL, potentially influencing the effectiveness of learning experiences for students. Prior to teaching SRL, it's essential to understand our own beliefs, interact with the given information to potentially experience cognitive conflict, and undergo a transformative process towards adopting beliefs that support the effective teaching of SRL. This ensures a foundation of inner beliefs to enhance our teaching practice about SRL.

Chapter summary

This chapter explored the different components of the concept of SRL. With this clarification of what SRL is, you can now more readily differentiate between SRL and other terms such as meta-learning, self-directed learning and metacognition, ensuring that when you speak about SRL with your students you can do so with confidence. Additionally, you now recognise there is a complex body of knowledge that underpins a student's SRL that is both situation and subject specific, meaning that your classroom context is an important place for the teaching of SRL. Given this deeper understanding, I wonder, as per the quote at the beginning of this chapter, have you changed the way you look at students' SRL?

Take action

- Facilitate an 'activating prior knowledge about SRL' activity with your students. If 'SRL' is not a term they are familiar with, consider using a synonym such as self-management.
- Ask your students: what does it mean to be a self-regulated learner? This is an opportunity to contribute some of the information and research that I have offered you in this chapter into a discussion with your class.
- To help your students develop their understanding of SRL, consider showing them my TEDx Talk, 'What we fail to learn in schools: self-regulated learning' (perhaps the first half as this relates to conceptualising SRL, whereas the second half relates to teaching SRL).
- Reflect on your own beliefs about SRL and consider how you might shift limiting beliefs to better enable the teaching of SRL in your classroom.

Delve deeper

My website **shyambarr.com/book** includes links to the following resources so you can explore the concepts in this chapter further.

- ☐ Watch my TEDx Talk and leave a comment indicating your biggest takeaway.
- ☐ Listen to the *Educate to Self-Regulate* podcast episode 2: 'What is SRL? What role does motivation play in the process of SRL?'
- ☐ Watch my 'Defining Metacognition' video.
- ☐ Read Lawson et al.'s (2018) paper 'Teachers' and Students' Belief Systems About the Self-Regulation of Learning'.

SRL TOOLBOX

Compare and contrast

By comparing and contrasting information, we can identify gaps in our understanding and align our prior knowledge with new information. This process is crucial in conceptualising SRL as it challenges our preconceived notions and builds a more robust framework for understanding.

Consider the similarities and differences between the information you generated as part of the 'activating prior knowledge' SRL toolbox activity at the end of chapter 1, and the information you have now explored in this chapter.

Did your prior conceptions acknowledge that:

- SRL is an umbrella term for a broad set of knowledge and skills?
- SRL is an active process of planning, monitoring and evaluating?
- SRL is the metacognitive changing (or 'regulating') of learning?
- SRL is a decision-making process and a daily practice?
- SRL is both domain-specific and general?

Applying the strategy in the classroom

Guide your students through a reflective exercise where they examine their previous understanding of SRL against the concepts discussed in class. Encourage them to:

- List down their initial thoughts about SRL.
- Compare those thoughts with the detailed characteristics of SRL discussed in this chapter.
- Identify similarities that reinforce their understanding and differences that offer new insights.
- Share their reflections with peers to broaden their perspective.

By critically analysing the two sets of information, students develop a deeper appreciation of the dynamic nature of SRL and the importance of tailoring learning strategies to specific contexts.

Transfer to other contexts

Consider how this strategy might be beneficial in learning other concepts. How could comparing and contrasting be used to deepen understanding in different academic disciplines or real-world scenarios?

PART II
Instructional approaches for developing SRL

Balancing her practical teaching responsibilities, Alex seeks to understand and implement SRL strategies with her students. Her exploration leads her to a wealth of research, revealing tried-and-tested approaches to teaching SRL. She quickly realises that while the concept of teaching SRL seems straightforward, the actual implementation is a complex, nuanced process. To make it easier, she conceptualises it as three steps (see Figure 8).

Figure 8. The three steps to teaching SRL

Identify
students' point of challenge with SRL

Modify
teaching practice and classroom environment

Monitor
students' SRL progress

First, she must identify her students' SRL challenges by gathering information about their SRL knowledge, beliefs and skill sets. Second, she must modify her teaching practice and the classroom environment to support her students' points of challenge. Third, she must monitor how students respond, and how their SRL progresses.

Part II is structured to guide you through this nuanced journey, much like Alex's three-step 'identify, modify, monitor' process. However, in reality, all the approaches discussed in this part are designed to promote students' SRL.

Chapter 3 starts by helping you recognise different students' SRL needs. In Chapters 4 and 5 we delve into how to directly teach SRL concepts and strategies. Chapter 6 explores the role of metacognition in SRL, offering practical ways to prompt and develop this critical skill. Chapter 7 brings it all together by illustrating how to create an environment that nurtures and supports SRL.

Pre-commitment strategy

Pre-commitment is a strategy commonly used in health fields to help individuals attempting to recover from addictions such as alcoholism or gambling. For example, a recovering alcoholic might wish to spend more time with friends but will eliminate meeting friends in locations where alcohol is present – they'll go for a walk in a park rather than meeting at a bar.

Addictive behaviours can also manifest in learning – for example, continually picking up a phone to check notifications – so the premise of a pre-commitment strategy offers benefits to learning scenarios as well. By engaging a pre-commitment strategy, learners have a higher likelihood of being present in the learning process and achieving their learning goals.

To engage a pre-commitment strategy:

- Write down a sentence about your intention for this reading experience (e.g. I want to be fully present with this chapter for the next 30 minutes).
- Identify any barriers that might hinder you achieving your intention (e.g. a phone notification beeping).
- Activate suitable strategies to mitigate barriers (e.g. switch your phone on silent, or place it outside of the room).

Applying the strategy in the classroom

- Allocate time for students to write a pre-commitment at the start of a lesson or study session.
- Discuss common barriers to learning (e.g. distractions), and brainstorm ways to mitigate them.
- Encourage students to hold each other accountable to their commitments.

Measure the impact of the pre-commitment strategy with a reflection exercise after the learning session. Ask students to consider:

- Did they manage to stay focused on their intention?
- What distractions arose and how did their pre-commitments help?
- Would they change anything about their approach for future learning sessions?

Transfer to other contexts

Beyond education, consider how the pre-commitment strategy can be applied in various aspects of life, such as personal goals, workplace tasks or even social commitments. How might committing to specific intentions and mitigating barriers lead to more successful outcomes in these areas?

3
Identifying students' SRL level

A correct diagnosis is three-fourths the remedy.

– Mahatma Ghandi

Based on the conceptualisation of SRL offered in Part I, we – educators – have three goals when it comes to supporting our students to self-regulate their learning:

1. To help students become aware of themselves as learners and their learning processes.
2. To help students develop a wide repertoire of strategies to help them regulate their learning process.
3. To provide opportunities for students to practise SRL in their daily learning experiences.

There will likely be substantial variation in your students' SRL knowledge. While your aspiration is to help students develop a deep knowledge in each of the five areas of SRL (motivation, cognition, metacognition, resource management and emotion), it is important to recognise that students are starting at different points in their SRL journey. You can start by identifying or 'diagnosing' what your student's or class's most prominent SRL challenge is by first collecting information about their current state of SRL. In other words, to teach SRL, we must understand what conceptions and misconceptions about SRL students hold, and therefore what the appropriate entry point is for teaching students SRL.

In this chapter, I invite you to gather information about students' SRL, using the following approaches:

- Observe students' SRL behaviours (using evidence-informed criteria).
- Ask students about their SRL.
- Implement learning journals.
- Get students to think-aloud.
- Have students self-record their SRL strategies (or behaviours/actions).

All the above approaches can be easily implemented during lessons. I'll share whole-school approaches to assessing SRL (e.g. competency-based learning approaches, rubrics and an SRL questionnaire) in Chapters 8 and 9.

Observing students' SRL behaviours

You observe students' learning behaviours every day in your class. You can enhance the way you observe students' SRL by drawing on a set of evidence-informed behavioural indicators such as those listed in Table 7.

Table 7 documents an evolving list of SRL behavioural indicators, a checklist of the things that students do if they demonstrate SRL. It's a starting point for considering what SRL behaviours a student might currently be demonstrating (strengths) and those less evident (weaknesses, or opportunities for growth).

When using behaviour as an indicator of SRL, it's important to remember that SRL is an active process of planning, monitoring and evaluating, and that even with deep knowledge about SRL, a learner is engaged in a daily practice (refer Chapter 1). Not all students will display SRL behaviours at the same level or in the same way. It's important to observe patterns in behaviour over time, instead of relying on a single instance. For example, a student not showing SRL behaviours in a particular moment doesn't mean they lack SRL skills. They might have the skills but are not using them in your classroom if their goals differ from the goals you have set. This begs a conversation about the student's motivational drivers rather than their SRL skill set. In other words, we need to be curious about our students rather than jumping to judgement.

Table 7. Behavioural indicators for SRL

SRL category	SRL behavioural indicators	Sub-indicators
Metacognition	Self-planning	• Sets clear and achievable learning goals (written or verbal). • Breaks down long-term goals into smaller, manageable tasks. • Regularly reviews and adjusts their goals based on progress. • Selects suitable strategies to apply in their learning process.
Metacognition	Self-monitoring	• Tracks their progress and achievements. • Adjusts their strategies based on their self-assessment. • Identifies when they are struggling and seeks help or adjusts their approach. • Keeps a learning journal or log.
Metacognition	Self-evaluation	• Periodically assesses their own learning outcomes. • Recognises their achievements and identifies areas where improvement is needed. • Uses self-assessment to guide future learning. • Recognises mistakes/errors. • Learns from both successes and failures.
Metacognition	Reflective practice	• Regularly reflects on their learning experiences. • Identifies their strengths and weaknesses as a learner.
Motivation	Task initiation	• Begins tasks promptly without external prompting. • Can self-motivate and start working on assignments independently. • Maintains focus on tasks even in the absence of immediate rewards.
Motivation	Persistence	• Remains motivated even in the face of challenges. • Persists through difficult tasks and doesn't give up easily (through challenging circumstances). • Takes responsibility for their learning and outcomes.
Cognition	Study strategies (cognitive strategies)	• Adapts study strategies to the nature of the task. • Utilises a variety of study techniques, such as summarisation, elaboration and self-quizzing. • Demonstrates an understanding of effective learning strategies.

SRL category	SRL behavioural indicators	Sub-indicators
Resource management	Organisation	• Keeps study materials, notes and resources well-organised. • Plans and structures their work effectively. • Uses tools such as to-do lists and calendars to stay organised.
	Time management	• Creates a study schedule or timetable. • Prioritises tasks and allocates time effectively. • Resists procrastination and stays on schedule.
	Seeking help	• Asks for assistance when needed. • Utilises available resources, such as teachers, tutors or peers. • Values others' input and feedback.
	Utilising feedback	• Actively seeks and uses feedback to enhance their learning. • Is open to constructive criticism and uses it to refine their work. • Makes adjustments based on feedback received.
Emotion	Task and/or test anxiety	• Recognises signs of anxiety and employs strategies to manage it. • Prepares thoroughly, which reduces anxiety related to testing. • Maintains a positive mindset and uses affirmations to stay calm during tests. • Utilises relaxation techniques such as deep breathing or visualisation before and during tests.
	Stress management	• Identifies sources of stress related to learning and takes proactive steps to address them. • Adopts healthy habits such as regular exercise and sufficient sleep to manage stress. • Practises time management to prevent last-minute stress due to deadlines. • Engages in relaxation or recreational activities to balance study and downtime. • Seeks support from peers or counsellors when overwhelmed by study-related stress.

ADAPTED FROM BARR (2021) AND DU ET AL. (2023).

Observing behaviour alone may not fully capture students' SRL accurately, as it overlooks the influence of their knowledge and beliefs about SRL. To garner a more informed evaluation of students' SRL, you can combine observation with assessment approaches that consider the internal cognitive processes – their thinking – that underpins SRL.

Asking students about their SRL

One of the simplest ways to gain insights into students' knowledge and beliefs about SRL is to ask them. For example, during a lesson, in an interaction with a student or the class, you might inject a question about an SRL concept or strategy. Examples can be found in Table 8.

Table 8. Examples of questions to ask students about their SRL

Question prompt	Example
What do you do when [x] occurs?	• What do you do when you're faced with a challenge? • What do you do when you feel a reading or task is too complex?
What strategies do you use to achieve [x]? What strategies do you use when doing [x]?	• What do you use to help you persist when something is challenging? • What is your go-to strategy to motivate yourself? • What strategy do you engage when experiencing high cognitive load? • What strategies do you use when comprehending text, problem-solving or writing an essay?
List five strategies that you use to do [x].	• List five strategies that you use to motivate yourself when starting a new task.
What have you tried already? What haven't you tried? What could you do?	• What have you tried already to solve this problem? What haven't you tried? What could you do?
What do you know about SRL?	• What does it mean to self-regulate your learning? • What does it look like when someone self-regulates their learning?

Teachers can seamlessly integrate these questions (Table 8) into student discussions and reflections about learning.

Whether you're using the questions documented in Table 8 or getting a class to share their strategies for common learning tasks, the following questioning strategies can help delve deeper into a student's SRL process:

- Asking for reasoning: 'What makes you say that?'
- Encouraging elaboration: 'Tell me some more about that.'
- Probing further with a sequence of 'Why?' questions.
- Clarifying student thoughts by paraphrasing: 'It sounds like…'
- Acknowledging their points by echoing back what they've said.

These questions serve as a diagnostic tool, shedding light on students' existing knowledge of SRL and revealing any misconceptions, which can then be addressed before new material is introduced. Take the time to carefully examine students' responses. Do your students have a sound understanding of themselves as learners and of their learning processes? Do your students have a broad and deep repertoire of effective strategies to help them self-regulate their learning in different learning contexts?

Implementing learning journals

Learning journals are personal diaries in which students document their thoughts, experiences and insights about their learning process. They offer a greater level of psychological safety than open conversations and may draw out more honest insights about SRL.

A key part of SRL is self-monitoring, where students reflect on their learning progress and strategies. Learning journals are a great tool for this. Dignath et al. (2023) looked into how effective learning journals are for improving things such as academic achievement, SRL and motivation. They reviewed 32 studies involving 3492 participants in total. Their findings showed that learning journals positively impact learning outcomes and SRL, but their effectiveness is dependent on how they are designed and used in the classroom. To help you embed learning journals in your classroom, I offer you an approach in Table 9.

Table 9 shows a way to use learning journals. I suggest giving students specific questions to answer in their journals. For example:

- What are my specific learning goals, and how do they align with the overall objectives of this course or activity?
- Which strategies were most effective for me in understanding and retaining the material, and how can I improve my approach to learning?

- How do I monitor my progress towards achieving my learning goals, and how can I make this process more effective?
- What challenges did I encounter during my learning process, and how did I address them?
- How can I apply what I've learned to future assignments, projects, or real-life situations?

Table 9. Approach to implementing learning journals in your classroom

Step	Action
1.	**Explain and discuss the term 'journalling' and establish current use of journals with students.** 'Raise your hand if you journal. Can anyone describe to the class what journalling is?'
2.	**Introduce learning journals by clearly defining the objectives of using them.** 'Today I want to share with you a type of journal known as a learning journal. Take a moment to write down what you think a learning journal might entail given our conversation about journalling.' Discuss. Learning journals are personal diaries where you can document your thoughts, experiences and insights about your learning process. It's a form of reflective practice that helps us develop greater self-awareness. We'll start practising this strategy in a physical notebook as the act of handwriting slows our thinking and can aid reflection.'
3.	**Model how to complete a learning journal.** For instance, you might show an exemplar or demonstrate how you complete a learning journal entry. 'When journalling, I use question prompts to help facilitate my reflections. - What have I learned? - How did I go about learning it? - What worked? - What didn't work?'
4.	**Establish psychological safety.** Who will view the learning journal? Student? Peers? Teacher? Parents? Please note students' willingness to share in a learning journal may depend on the potential readers. 'What you write will only be read by yourself and me (the teacher) so that I can provide feedback on your learning process and strategies; however, at times, I'll ask you to draw on your reflections in your learning journals in group sharing. It's important that we feel safe in writing about our learning process.'

Step	Action
5	**Provide students an opportunity to practise journalling about their learning.** Hand out notebooks* and invite students to make a journal entry. I suggest a daily practice of 5–15 minutes to build this reflective habit. * Ensure accessibility based on available resources and technological infrastructure. Physical journals or digital journals? (If opting for digital diaries, ensure that students can easily access these digital tools.)
6	**Reflect on strategy and activate transfer.** 'Now that you've made your first journal entry, let's reflect on the experience. How did it feel to write about your learning process? Discussing our journalling experience helps us understand our learning strategies and how we can apply them in different areas. Next, think about how you can use this reflection in other subjects or outside school to enhance your learning.'
7	**Periodically review and provide feedback on the learning journal entries.** Feedback on students' entries along with an opportunity for learners to revise their reflections has been shown to yield higher effects for SRL (Dignath et al., 2023). 'Every two weeks, I'll collect the learning journals to review your entries. I'll focus on the content, the depth of reflection and the learning strategies you've used. After my review, you'll get a chance to revise your reflections based on the feedback.'

Using prompts to guide journal entries has been found to be more effective (such as in the study by Nückles et al., 2004) than open entries. You can use the same questions each time or change them up to draw out different information from students about their learning approach.

As students increase their competence with journalling and become better at reflecting on their learning, gradually remove scaffolding (e.g. questions or prompts) and allow them to freely reflect on their learning. You can offer them some freedom in how they write their journals, including the choice of format, what they write about and how deeply they reflect. However, be cautious with less structured learning journals. If students don't understand their importance or take them seriously, they might make entries that are inappropriate or frivolous, offering little insight into their learning capabilities.

Getting students to think-aloud

Another way to gain insight into students thinking is to get them to think-aloud. For those unfamiliar with the approach, thinking-aloud requires individuals to vocalise their thoughts, feelings and cognitive processes while performing a task, offering educators valuable insights into students' SRL. Thinking-aloud offers numerous benefits. When students articulate their thoughts during a learning task, they become more aware of their learning process. When students' thinking is visible, educators can then identify misconceptions and provide feedback about SRL. It's a common process in research and classrooms, but not always implemented in a way that is optimal for students' SRL. To get students thinking-aloud to enhance SRL, try the approach in Table 10.

Table 10. Approach to implementing think-aloud protocols in your classroom

Step	Action
1.	**Choose a task.** Select a learning activity or problem that is challenging yet manageable for students to think-aloud.
2.	**Teach the think-aloud strategy.** 'Today, we'll learn about the think-aloud strategy, a powerful tool for SRL. Thinking-aloud involves verbalising what you're thinking as you think it. It helps generate awareness about our thinking processes which helps us make better decisions about our learning. In a moment, I'll demonstrate a think-aloud while solving a problem. I encourage you to ask questions at any point for clarity. Remember, the goal is to make your mental process transparent, offering a window into your thinking as you engage with a learning task.'
3.	**Establish a supportive environment for thinking-aloud.** 'To make our classroom a safe space for sharing our thoughts, let's set clear expectations and outcomes for thinking-aloud. First, hearing someone else's thought process is a privilege and should be treated with respect. Second, there's no judgement here – mistakes are simply part of the learning process.'
4.	**Provide structured prompts.** 'To help you think-aloud, start by asking yourself, [teacher selects appropriate questions] "What is the problem I am trying to solve?" Follow up with, "What do I already know about this topic?" and "What strategies can I use here?" After attempting a solution, reflect with "Why did this approach work or not work?" and "What could I try differently next time?" Using these structured prompts will help you to methodically navigate through your thinking process and articulate it more clearly, which is essential for developing your SRL skills.'

Step	Action
5.	**Practise think-alouds with transcription support.** There are several ways to practise think-alouds: • With students in pairs, one thinks aloud as they complete the task, the other provides feedback (promotes collaborative learning and an opportunity for peer-learning) – they could practise individually or together. • Individual students think-aloud with teacher (or, if comfortable, in front of class). • Students record their think-alouds on a phone or laptop while completing a learning activity, and then use a transcription program (e.g. otter.ai) and annotate their transcribed think-aloud – acknowledging the planning, monitoring and evaluating phases, or highlighting any strategies that emerge during their SRL process. 'During think-aloud practice, you can use a transcription program to record and print out your thoughts. This tool, which we'll learn to use together, will help you see your thinking process on paper. Afterwards, you can annotate your transcript to highlight the planning, monitoring and evaluating stages of your problem-solving, as well as any strategies you've used. This visual reflection will allow us to recognise our learning patterns and improve our SRL process.'
6.	**Regularly assess and provide feedback on think-alouds.** 'At regular intervals, I will review your think-aloud practices assessing the clarity and depth of your verbalisations, how you correct any errors, and the way you reflect on your thinking. This will help me give you constructive feedback to guide your progress. I encourage you to also look at your own think-aloud recordings or transcriptions to self-assess and identify areas for improvement. By doing this, you can set personal goals to enhance your thinking and learning process, further developing your SRL skills.'

Is this approach to thinking-aloud prominent in your classroom? Could your approach to thinking-aloud be enhanced by incorporating aspects listed in Table 10? How might you tweak your approach to better illuminate students' process of self-regulated learning?

Please note that performing a think-aloud while engaged in a learning activity is a dual task and may create extraneous cognitive load (additional pressure on working memory), potentially affecting how a student performs a task or the quality of verbalisation. Additionally, some students may be unaware of their thinking processes that underly certain learning behaviours. Both extraneous cognitive load and lack of awareness can be mitigated through effective training of learners in how to complete a think-aloud.

When students think-aloud, look out for the:

- Quality of students' metacognitive self-talk:
  - Quality of students' self-instructions (what they tell themselves)
  - Quality of students' self-questions (what they ask themselves)
- Quality of students' strategy use during learning.

Inviting students to self-record their SRL

Another way to glean insights into students' SRL in the classroom is to have them self-record their own SRL behaviours. Self-recording is a key component of both the monitoring and evaluating phases of SRL, and self-recording interventions have been shown to enhance students' awareness of their behaviours, leading to greater SRL capabilities (e.g. Smith et al., 2022). Self-recording can take many forms, but the central idea is that a learner is recording the frequency of a certain behaviour.

Let's look at an example of a self-recording strategy often used to develop awareness of attention: the tally strategy.

My co-host on the *Educate to Self-Regulate* podcast, Rory McCaughey, and I worked together on self-recording methods in his classroom. Through this, Rory created a simple technique called the tally strategy. This approach helps students keep track of their attention and manage distractions by making tallies. Table 11 lists the steps involved in facilitating the tally strategy with your students.

Table 11. Steps to implement the tally strategy

Step	Action
1.	**Set up materials.** Hand out a post-it note to each student.
2.	**Introduce self-recording and define off-task behaviours.** 'Today, we're going to do a little experiment to help us gather information about our attention. We'll use a self-recording technique. Have you heard of self-recording? Self-recording is a technique used to help us generate awareness about our own behaviours. Today, we're going to self-record our attention when we're off-task.' Clarify what on-task versus off-task behaviours are, with examples.

Step	Action
3.	**Explain the act of keeping a tally strategy.** 'Whenever you notice your off-task, in that moment when you realise you're off task, I want you to make a check on your post-it note (i.e. add a check to your tally). What are some off-task behaviours that might happen? Daydreaming? Distracted by a friend? Distracted by technology?...'
4.	**Teach self-instruction techniques.** 'In that moment of realisation I want you to gently guide your attention to the learning task, by saying to yourself "be present" or 'focus on the task".'
5.	**Create a non-competitive environment.** 'This exercise is not a competition, it's just about gathering information about our attention and how it functions.'
6.	**Allow for self-recording practice.** Students practise self-recording while completing a learning activity or during a lesson.
7.	**Allow for reflection and goal-setting.** At the end of the activity/lesson, have students reflect on their tallies and share strategies that helped them refocus. 'Take a moment now to reflect on your tallies. What do you notice about your attention? What happened today? Why do you think that happened? Did self-recording your attention support your focus? What might you do to reduce your off-task behaviours next time?'
8.	**Inspire transfer of skills.** 'Would you use the tally strategy again? What other aspects of learning and life might we self-record?'

Identifying your students' points of challenge

Gathering information about students' SRL does not need to be an arduous process. The approaches listed are easily weaved into regular lessons. Simply make note of any observation and student statements that provide an insight into their SRL. If you wish, you can collect work samples, student reflections or learning journals to more formally review students' SRL knowledge and behaviours.

Once you have gathered information about your students' SRL, contrast the information gathered against the behavioural indicators in Table 7, or use the SRL knowledge framework (Figure 3) and identify whether each learner's challenge is motivational, cognitive, metacognitive or related to resource management or emotional regulation. In other words, and with a better understanding of your students' current SRL, it's time to consider: what is getting in the way of your students better self-regulating their learning?

Identifying students' specific challenges with SRL is crucial in tailoring educational approaches effectively. Through this exercise we can pinpoint whether a student lacks SRL skills or simply struggles to employ them correctly – Veenman's (2017) production or availability deficiencies. When a student does not have particular SRL skills – a production deficiency – explicit instruction becomes necessary (we'll discuss this further in Chapters 4 and 5). This involves explicit teaching of the strategies and skills involved in SRL. In contrast, if the student has the skills but fails to use them properly (availability deficiency), then what is needed is prompting: cues or questions that nudge students to apply their SRL skills appropriately (Chapter 6). Once we are clear on what the student's point of challenge is, we can better decide the appropriate teaching intervention.

Chapter summary

This chapter provided teaching approaches to gather information about students' SRL. It advocated for moving beyond observation of students' SRL behaviours, to incorporate measures that explores students' thinking processes – learning journals, thinking-aloud and self-recording – illuminating their knowledge and beliefs about SRL. Collectively, these methods equip you with a multifaceted approach to understand students' strengths and weaknesses with SRL and to pinpoint students' most prominent challenge with SRL. This forms the foundation for deciding an appropriate teaching intervention.

Take action

- Provide students with the list of behavioural indicators (Table 7) and have them reflect on their own SRL. You could get them to rate themselves on a simple five-point Likert scale for each of the behaviours. You can also ask them to observe each other and provide feedback on their SRL behaviours.
- Ask your students about their SRL (e.g. how they went about learning something, what strategies they use when they are lacking motivation

and so on). Consider using a focused conversation tool, such as the 2 × 10 strategy, whereby you engage in a two-minute conversation with a selected learner for ten consecutive days. An alternative strategy is to have a list of students and mark off each student as you engage in a conversation with them, ensuring that you speak with all your students.

- Ask your class to write about the best ways to go about understanding information, solving particular problems or writing an essay. Consider the details of the students' responses. It is likely that you will see quite a range of knowledge about how to carry out these very common learning activities.
- Implement a learning journal approach. Choose an approach based on the SRL competence of your students – for example, if your students are relatively new to SRL, provide guiding questions to scaffold their learning journal entries. If your students are progressing well with their SRL, consider more unstructured forms of journalling and focus on different approaches to journalling.
- Get students to think-aloud before, during and after a learning process.
- Invite students to self-record particular SRL behaviours (or non-SRL behaviours). For example, you may like to implement the tally strategy to help students develop awareness of their attention regulating capabilities.

Delve deeper

My website **shyambarr.com/book** includes links to the following resources so you can explore the concepts in this chapter further.

- ☐ Explore Evidence for Learning's website resources covering metacognition and SRL, including the 'red amber green' assessment tool.
- ☐ Read the blog article: '3 Steps to becoming a better listener...' to help you deeply listen to your students' SRL.
- ☐ Read the blog article: 'Enhance your reflective practice with this simple tool' for a simple reflective protocol that you can use to semi-structure a learning journal.

Empathy mapping

Empathy mapping is a strategy that is often used in user experience (UX) design, design thinking and human-centred design (Matthews & Wrigley, 2017). Product designers use empathy mapping to understand their end user before creating a product (e.g. empathising with a five-year-old when creating a toy for kindergarten/preschool). After discovering empathy mapping and using it with my Years 7 and 8 Science classes, I realised that empathy mapping could also be used as a reflection tool and a goal-setting strategy, addressing two phases of SRL: planning and evaluating.

To engage in empathy mapping:

- Think of a student who is not self-regulating their learning very well.
- Take an A3 sheet of paper and divide it in half by drawing a line down the middle or folding it in half.
- On one side of the paper, draw a Y-chart with three sections labelled 'Thinking,' 'Feeling' and 'Saying/Doing'.
- Consider the student in their current state and fill in each section of the chart with observations and inferences about what the student is thinking and feeling, and what they might say or do as a result of these thoughts and feelings.
- Extension: as a goal-setting strategy, on the other side of the folded paper envision the student in a future state where they are effectively self-regulating their learning and repeat the exercise from this perspective.

Applying the strategy in the classroom

- Introduce empathy mapping to students as a way to reflect on their learning processes and set goals.

- Encourage students to create their own empathy maps for self-reflection.
- Use empathy maps in teacher-student conferences to discuss barriers to learning and to collaboratively set goals for improvement.

Transfer to other contexts

Consider using empathy mapping to get students to empathise with famous individuals involved in different learning contexts (e.g. Sam Kerr as a professional sportsperson; Albert Einstein). What might that famous individual think, feel, say and do when confronted with a learning challenge or when seeking a particular learning outcome?

4
Explicit teaching approaches to promote SRL

> Knowledge is power.
>
> – Sir Francis Bacon

In the context of SRL, the adage 'knowledge is power' holds true. This is because a learner's depth of understanding about their own learning process is fundamental to their SRL. Such understanding not only drives their engagement in learning but also significantly influences their academic achievements. As you know, we can teach students how to become self-regulated learners. In this chapter, I invite you to:

- explicitly teach SRL concepts and strategies
- consider findings from classroom observation studies
- clarify the differences between implicit and explicit SRL instruction
- move from implicit to explicit teaching of SRL strategies, using the NEMO-T approach
- integrate NEMO-T into student conversations
- incorporate interactive dialogue about SRL.

Explicit teaching of SRL concepts and strategies

Explicit teaching of SRL strategies in both primary and secondary settings involves creating learning experiences where students deepen their knowledge about SRL, including SRL strategies. Teaching SRL strategies can occur in different ways; refer Figure 9.

Figure 9. Four modes of instructing SRL strategies

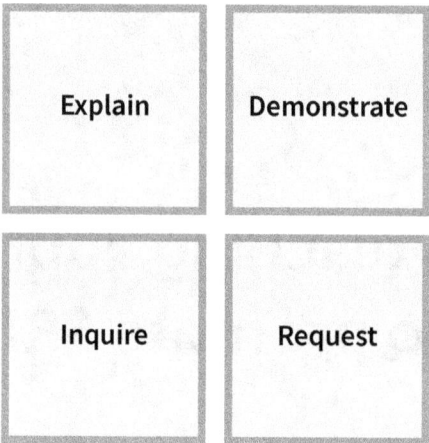

ADAPTED FROM DIGNATH ET AL. (2022).

When it comes to explicitly teaching SRL strategies, particularly introducing a strategy for the first time, it is important to **explain** how the strategy functions, including:

- what the strategy is
- how to use the strategy
- when and why to use the strategy.

An explanation that incorporates the *what* (declarative knowledge), the *how* (procedural knowledge) and the *when* and *why* (conditional knowledge) of a strategy, ensures students' foster the knowledge to effectively apply the strategy to support learning.

You can also **demonstrate** to students how to use a strategy, setting out the individual steps involved to action a strategy. I position these two modes at the top of Figure 9, as a more knowledgeable other (e.g. a teacher or another student) is sharing knowledge of SRL strategies with students. Additionally, you can **inquire** about students' strategy use by asking students what strategies they use, how they use them and when and why they use them. Or you can **request** that students use a specific strategy during a learning task. The two modes of inquire and request are positioned on the same level in Figure 9 as they require students to have knowledge of strategies and to be able to share their knowledge or apply it upon request.

When combined, the four modes – explain, demonstrate, inquire and request – can be an effective method to teaching SRL strategies.

Do you explicitly teach SRL strategies in your classroom?
What mode or modes do you typically use?
Is it common practice at your school?

At this point, you might be reflecting on aspects of your practice where you already explicitly teach SRL strategies. This reflection is important as it indicates you making connections between what you're reading and your own practice. However, be aware that your instruction of SRL strategies might be more implicit than explicit, as suggested by numerous studies over the past two decades.

Findings from classroom observation studies

Multiple classroom observation studies have indicated that while teachers may teach SRL strategies, this is more often than not, done in an implicit way, rather than an explicit way (refer Dignath and colleagues, e.g. Dignath & Büttner, 2008; Dignath and Büttner, 2018; Dignath & Veenman, 2021). My own research here in Australia has also demonstrated that educators spend very little time explicitly teaching SRL strategies in primary and secondary classrooms (Barr, 2021; 2022b). For example, in a classroom observation study of eight middle leaders' teaching practice about SRL, analysing 25 videoed lessons, middle leaders spent less than two minutes per 45 minute lesson explicitly teaching SRL strategies (Barr, 2022b). That's less than 4 per cent of the lesson spent explicitly teaching SRL strategies. Figure 10 (overleaf) shows the average number of minutes teachers in the study spent on teaching SRL strategies.

Figure 10. Analysis of strategy instruction from 25 video-recorded lesson observations in an Australian secondary school

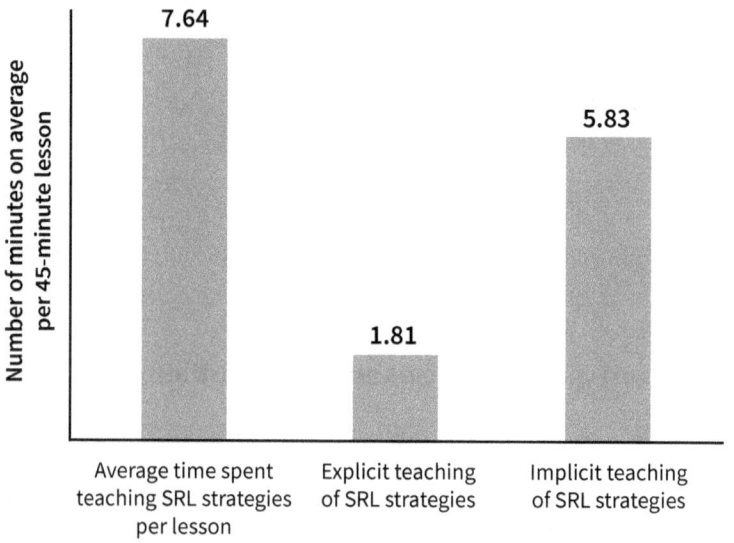

BARR, 2022B.

Figure 10 demonstrates, similar to the other research cited in this section, that educators spend more time implicitly rather than explicitly teaching SRL strategies. It seems there might be a disconnect between:

- what we think we do (**explicitly** teach SRL concepts and strategies – based on our perceptions and what teachers tell me) and
- what we actually do (**implicitly** teach SRL concepts and strategies - based on classroom observation studies).

Where do you think your SRL teaching typically sits? Explicit? Implicit? A combination?

It is important to note that this is not a matter of adding yet another thing – self-regulated learning – to your teaching workload. Rather, I'm suggesting that our greatest opportunity lies not in adding new things, but being smarter with the things we're already doing. In other words, if we maximise the seven or so minutes that we're already spending in a 45 minute lesson, by shifting the implicit to explicit, then we optimise the chances of our students developing their SRL skill set. While nothing is guaranteed, we can walk away from our lessons knowing that we did the best that we could do with the most up-to-date research to inform our practice.

Differences between implicit and explicit SRL instruction

To help you further understand the differences between explicit and implicit SRL instruction, refer to Table 12.

Table 12. Explicit versus implicit strategy instruction

Four modes of instructing SRL strategy	Explicit strategy instruction	Implicit strategy instruction
Explain	Teacher provides information about the strategy and how it functions, including its timing and procedural steps, and may provide examples. 'I want you to think about the goals you want to set for this lesson. The naming of goals is actually a strategy to help you learn better in the future. Now it's about motivating yourself. Whenever you don't feel like working or you are too tired, you should think about the goals you have set. And that should motivate you to actually do what you have set out to do.'	Teacher's explanation of a strategy is unclear or information about the strategy is convoluted by task instructions. In some cases, students are left to seek information about a strategy from other sources (e.g. a textbook, worksheets). 'Make sure you take notes as we watch *Othello*.' In this instance, the teacher loosely mentions the strategy of note-taking but provides no explanation of how to take effective notes.
Demonstrate	Teacher exhibits the use of a particular SRL strategy by explicitly pointing it out. They show the students how to apply the strategy and provide an explanation about it. 'I'll show you on the board how to apply this strategy to the text problem. First you write down what is wanted. Then what is given…'	Teacher applies a strategy without explicitly mentioning it. They demonstrate the strategy without pointing it out or explaining it. The teacher writes on the board: 'What is wanted? What is given?' However, the teacher does not say that this is a strategy, and that this strategy makes it easier to solve text problems.

Four modes of instructing SRL strategy	Explicit strategy instruction	Implicit strategy instruction
Inquire	The teacher asks the students if/how/when/why they have applied certain strategies in order to develop knowledge about strategies and their application. 'Alex, what can you do in this task so that you can solve it more easily? … Exactly, you can write down what is wanted, what is given. How do you come up with that now? … Right, we learned that yesterday. And what is it good for?'	Teacher does not ask explicit questions about a strategy or its application. However, the topic/problem refers implicitly to a certain strategy. 'And when you start with the text problem, first think about what could help you to solve them more easily. We learned something about that yesterday.'
Request	Teacher invites students to use a particular strategy during a learning task. 'Today, I want you all to use the [x] strategy which will help you solve these text problems more easily in the next assignments.'	Teacher reminds the students to apply a certain strategy without explicitly requesting they use the strategy. Nevertheless, the hint implicates an unexpressed request. 'Today, independently calculate these tasks. You know how to do it.'

ADAPTED FROM DIGNATH ET AL. (2022, PP. 9–12), WITH PERMISSION.

In other words, during implicit teaching of SRL strategies, a teacher might allude to students using a strategy without explaining when or why the strategy is applicable. The intent to teach a strategy is not made apparent to students, nor is metacognitive reflection encouraged.

During explicit teaching of SRL, a teacher would teach an SRL strategy with clear directions about the application, monitoring and evaluation of the strategy. In this instance, teachers will likely use the term 'strategy' and explain its use and benefits, often accompanied by metacognitive reflection.

Can you more clearly see the difference between explicit and implicit approaches to teaching SRL?

Is there scope for you to be more explicit in your SRL instruction? To be more deliberate and almost systematically incorporate SRL instruction into your classroom?

Implicit to explicit teaching of SRL strategies, using the NEMO-T approach

To enhance your explicit SRL instruction, you can use the acronym 'NEMO-T' when teaching SRL strategies. Refer Figure 11.

Figure 11. The NEMO-T approach for teaching SRL strategies

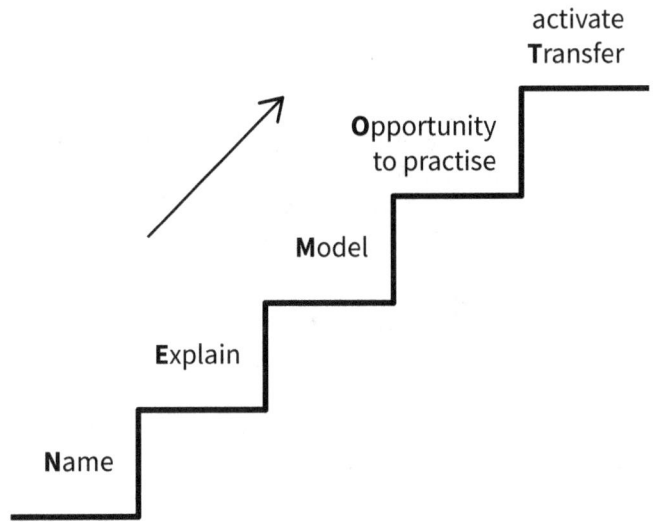

To apply the NEMO-T approach, you **name** the strategy, **explain** what the strategy is and why it's useful (i.e. the benefits), **model** how to use the strategy, provide students with an **opportunity** to practise using the SRL strategy, and then **activate transfer** for when and how the strategy might be used in other learning contexts. To help you further understand how NEMO-T is applied in context, I use the tally strategy as an example; refer Table 13.

Table 13. NEMO-T applied to the teaching of the tally strategy

NEMO-T approach	NEMO-T applied to the tally strategy
Name the strategy.	'Today I'm going to share with you a metacognitive strategy called self-recording.'
Explain what the strategy is.	'Self-recording is a strategy to help develop an awareness of a certain behaviour. For example, often when you start at a gym, a trainer might ask you to keep a food diary – this is a form of self-recording, in that each day for a period of time, you record what you eat. Similarly, studies conducted with smokers have shown that when individuals self-recorded how many cigarettes they smoked per day, they reduced the number of cigarettes they smoked.'
Model how to use the strategy.	'I'm going to show you how to self-record your on-task and off-task behaviours using the tally strategy. Let's create a table with the different off-task behaviours along the left-hand side. Now, during today's lesson, every time you notice yourself engaged in an off-task behaviour, I want you to make a tally in the appropriate box on the right-hand side. In essence, you will self-record when you are off-task. Once you have made your tally, I want you to return to the task (i.e. on-task behaviours).' Then facilitate a discussion with students about what on-task and off-task behaviours look like.
Provide an **opportunity** for students to practise.	Allow the students to practise the new strategy during a meaningful task.
Activate **transfer**.	Discuss with students how they might use self-recording, such as the tally strategy, in other learning situations and contexts. 'How might you use the tally strategy to self-record other aspects of your learning? Would this be useful in other subjects? What about outside of school?'

Please note, explicit teaching of SRL strategies (e.g. using the NEMO-T approach) does not mean the teaching needs to be highly didactic (teacher-centred, rote learning, copious slideshows, etc.), but that in moments of instruction, we are explicit about the SRL strategies that can progress learning.

Integrating NEMO-T into student conversations

Imagine that you notice a student appears 'stuck' and does not seem to be applying SRL strategies that have been explicitly taught using the NEMO-T approach (name, explain, model, opportunity, activate transfer) we discussed in Chapter 4. What questions will you ask to get your student to reflect on their learning and generate the previously taught strategy or another strategy? Let's take a look at an example of how the conversation might play out (adapted from Vosniadou et al., 2021, p. 37).

Imagine yourself as the teacher in this scenario:

Teacher: 'How's it going?'

Student: 'I'm confused. I don't know what to do now?'

Teacher: 'Okay, let's talk through your process – what have you tried?'

Student: [Responds.]

Teacher: 'Hmmm … can you think of any other ways you could consider this problem?'

Student: 'Maybe I could …' [This might be sufficient so student realises and moves on], or 'I don't know.'

Teacher: [If the student indicates 'I don't know'] Do you remember the X strategy? I would like you to apply the X strategy that we discussed in class last week.

If the student is still unclear at this point, you could use the NEMO-T approach to explicitly teach the strategy again.

Alternatively, depending on the classroom culture and the level of psychological safety, you might make this a classroom discussion:

Teacher: Okay, let's just pause here for a moment. I'd like you to share with us how you have been working on this problem, so we can think about it together.

Students: [Discuss approaches]

Teacher: [If no suitable approach is arrived at, offer students an approach]

You can prompt the student to retrieve their own SRL knowledge or to seek suggestions from the class (allowing other students to retrieve their SRL knowledge). If no suitable response is found, then it informs you, as the teacher, that your students do not have adequate SRL knowledge to navigate such challenges, hindering their ability to engage in SRL. You can teach them the appropriate SRL strategy once again.

You could also ask students to explain how they learn (individually or as a group):

- How did you do that?
- How did you solve that problem?
- How did you get that correct answer? (Vosniadou et al., 2021)

By asking these questions in a whole-class scenario, you are essentially having students explicitly acknowledge the strategies that they used to make progress and achieve success, allowing students with less effective strategies to benefit from others' teaching. Ensure that when students are sharing their strategies you repeat and reframe their explanation using NEMO-T to benefit weaker students.

Incorporating interactive dialogue about SRL

You can also incorporate interactive dialogue about SRL in the classroom to help students develop their knowledge of SRL strategies. Using Chi and Wylie's (2014) Interactive-Constructive-Active-Passive (ICAP) framework, we can consider the quality of different modes of learning engagement for SRL. Refer Table 14.

Table 14. Examples of SRL activities by mode of engagement

Passive (Receiving)	Active (Manipulating)	Constructive (Generating)	Interactive (Dialoguing)
Listening to a teacher explain the principles of SRL without taking notes or questioning the content.	Taking notes during an SRL lesson or highlighting strategies in a text about SRL.	Summarising an article on SRL strategies or creating a mind map to connect various SRL concepts.	Engaging in a group discussion to question and refine understanding of SRL strategies or teaching peers about your personalised SRL approach.

ADAPTED FROM CHI & WYLIE'S (2014) ICAP FRAMEWORK.

Interactive dialogue encourages students to articulate their thoughts, ask questions and explain concepts to peers, fostering deeper cognitive engagement. Some further examples of interactive dialogue in the context of learning about SRL include:

- **Debate:** Students could engage in a structured debate regarding the efficacy of different SRL strategies, which would require them to articulate their understanding of SRL, listen to and critique the perspectives of others and defend their viewpoints.
- **Role-playing:** In a role-play scenario, students could act out various approaches to SRL in different study situations, with classmates providing feedback on the strengths and weaknesses of each approach.
- **Peer teaching:** Students could pair up or form small groups to teach each other about various aspects of SRL, such as goal-setting or self-monitoring. This would involve discussing and questioning each other's understanding and strategies, fostering a deeper grasp of the concepts.

These interactive dialogues enable students to explore and consolidate their understanding of SRL by engaging with their peers, questioning assumptions and applying theory to practice.

Grouping students according to their SRL challenges or strengths can greatly enhance peer teaching and collaborative learning. For example, students grappling with the same SRL issue can collaborate to find solutions, while those who have excelled in particular SRL strategies can assist their peers. The integration of interactive dialogue about SRL should be timely: it is most effective when students are already familiar with the content, enabling them to actively participate in discussions and apply what they've learned. Such dialogue is also invaluable during complex tasks, where peer support can be pivotal, as well as during the reflection stage, where students assess and refine their SRL approaches and outcomes.

Chapter summary

By now, you recognise that one primary method for helping students to become self-regulated learners is to incorporate explicit opportunities for students to better understand SRL concepts and strategies. One useful teaching tool is the NEMO-T acronym: *name, explain, model, opportunity (to practise), (activate) transfer.* The acronym is easy to remember, and it allows you to engage in high-quality instruction of SRL strategies. Additionally, you can engage students in interactive dialogue with an explicit focus on SRL concepts or strategies, enabling students to co-construct their understanding of SRL. Remember, this is a not a matter of adding to teacher workload, but enhancing our practice to support students' SRL skill set.

Take action

- Explicitly teach SRL strategies using the NEMO-T approach.
- Based on your students' point of regulatory challenge (motivation, cognition, metacognition, emotion or resource management), identify one strategy that you could explicitly teach to your student (using the NEMO-T approach) to help them overcome their identified challenge.
- Incorporate opportunities for students to engage in interactive dialogue about different SRL concepts and strategies.

Delve deeper

My website **shyambarr.com/book** includes links to the following resources so you can explore the concepts in this chapter further.

- ☐ Watch my '4 strategies to dramatically uplevel students' SRL' video. Please leave a comment under the video with one thing that you learned or consolidated about teaching SRL.
- ☐ Read Vosniadou et al (2021) 'Teaching students how to learn: Setting the stage for lifelong learning'. Consider sections 3 and 4, pages 26–33.
- ☐ Read the 'Assessing how Teachers Enhance Self-Regulated Learning Coding Guide' (Dignath et al., 2022).

SRL TOOLBOX

Find a frontrunner

Observing a peer or slightly more advanced individual succeed can boost our self-efficacy. It shows that the skill is attainable and allows for learning nuanced skills that may not be captured in written or verbal instructions.

To find a frontrunner:

- Seek out someone who already has a focus on teaching SRL or someone you consider to be making good progress in their teaching SRL efforts.
- Approach them and ask them they would be willing to demonstrate their approach to you.
- Observe their teaching and ask questions to clarify any steps or techniques that are unclear.

Applying the strategy in the classroom

- Encourage students to view their classmates as resources in various tasks.
- Create a classroom culture where 'finding a frontrunner' is a common practice and students feel comfortable both offering and seeking help.
- Highlight and praise the use of the strategy to reinforce its value.
- Provide opportunities for students to demonstrate their skills to others, fostering a community of learning and expertise sharing.

Transfer to other contexts

How can this strategy be applied outside of school, such as in sports, hobbies, or future professions? What might a frontrunner look like in different contexts?

5
Incorporating SRL instruction into curriculum design

Teaching students how to learn within a particular domain is as crucial as the content itself.

— Dunlosky et al. (2013)

There are multiple ways to incorporate the NEMO-T approach and the four modes (explain, demonstrate, inquire and request) into your classroom. However, Lee et al. (2023) argued that SRL strategies be taught in context, combining subject-specific strategies with SRL strategies. For instance, in science, a student must have strategies to formulate hypotheses, design procedures and evaluate experiments. To do this effectively requires the student to also possess metacognitive strategies such as the different self-questions that are required to progress a scientific experiment (e.g. what do I think might happen? What elements make up an operational hypothesis?).

As another example, In art, a student requires strategies to generate ideas, create visual representations and refine these through critique and revision. To do this effectively requires the student to plan, monitor and evaluate their creative process using multiple metacognitive self-instructions, such as 'What's my goal? Am I on track? Do I require help?' and so on.

When SRL strategies are closely aligned with the subject context, they resonate more with students. This tailored approach helps students grasp the strategic knowledge more deeply and see its relevance and benefits in their learning journey. In essence, the specific strategies in each domain – be it science or art – foster a kind of learning that is both effective and meaningful for students in that particular subject.

In this chapter, I invite you to:

- set learning intentions and success criteria about SRL
- design a unit of inquiry and align to curriculum goals
- incorporate SRL strategy instruction into feedback conversations
- offer a course about SRL that has explicit transfer opportunities built in.

Set learning intentions and success criteria about SRL

Learning intentions and success criteria are well established in Australian education as having a positive influence on learning (AITSL, n.d.; Department of Education and Training, 2020). Learning intentions are 'descriptions of what learners should know, understand and be able to do by the end of a learning period' (AITSL, n.d.). Success criteria 'contain indicators and measures of skills, knowledge and understanding required to meet the learning [intentions]' (Wu & Goff, 2023, p. 412). Learning intentions and success criteria are used by educators and learners to facilitate goal-setting and provide clarity on the focus of the learning experience, enhance learner motivation and enable learners to actively engage in SRL (Department of Education and Training, 2020; William, 2017; William & Leahy, 2015). Learning intentions and success criteria about SRL require an explicit focus on knowledge, understanding and skills related to SRL. Refer Table 15 for examples of learning intentions and success criteria drawn from the Australian Curriculum's (V9; ACARA, 2024) Personal and Social Capability – Self-Management – Goal-setting – Level 5 (Years 7 and 8).

Table 15. Examples of learning intentions and success criteria about the metacognitive component of SRL

Learning intentions	Success criteria
Understand the role of goal-setting in the planning, monitoring and evaluating of learning (i.e. SRL).	I can explain how goals are connected to other phases of my learning, such as self-evaluation and processing feedback.
Understand examples of different goal-setting strategies and implications for learning.	I can apply different goal-setting strategies in my learning.

In 2022, Bonython Primary School focused on 'split screen learning intentions' (Murdoch, 2015) that covered both content knowledge and general capabilities, such as SRL, in lessons. However, educators were setting multiple learning intentions and success criteria for subject content knowledge and SRL, which was overwhelming for both teaching staff and students (cognitive load was high). I suggested focusing on a single learning intention and success criteria about SRL for a focused duration such as a series of lessons, a week or month, or even a unit or semester. As a result, one teaching team spent a whole unit focusing on self-talk. Refer Table 16 for an example of how this was planned.

Table 16. Example of Bonython Primary School teaching planner that highlights SRL focus for each week

Term/week	SRL focus
Term 1, Week 9	As a self-manager, how can positive self-talk help me as a learner?
Term 1, Week 10	As a self-manager, how can I maintain focus on my learning?
Term 2, Week 1	As a self-manager, how can I maintain focus on my learning?
Term 2, Week 2	As a self-manager, how can I reflect on my learning?
Term 2, Week 3	As a self-manager, how can I get feedback on my learning?
Term 2, Week 4	As a self-manager, how can I apply feedback?

Table 16 shows the different SRL focuses of lessons over several weeks. These weekly focuses were then translated into lesson goals, as depicted in Table 17.

Table 17. Example of lesson focus at Bonython Primary School (adapted)

What are we learning?	How are we learning?
What do writers do?	As a self-manager, how can I identify and use strategies to work towards my goal? • Looking back at old work • Not getting distracted or panicking • Get ideas from plan • Go over your writing and check

By incorporating an explicit focus on SRL, educators were able to elaborate on different SRL concepts and strategies in multiple lessons and in different contexts that not only supported students in developing their conceptual and strategic knowledge, but also supported transfer between different contexts.

Design a unit of inquiry and align to curriculum goals

You can also create a multidisciplinary unit with an SRL focus, providing structured opportunities for students to learn and develop SRL skills. For instance, Rory (a primary school educator from Melbourne Girls Grammar and my co-host on the *Educate to Self-Regulate* podcast) leads a Year 6, eight-week inquiry unit called 'Facing the Challenge'. The unit comprises six component parts, as depicted in Table 18.

Table 18. Implementing an inquiry unit that promotes SRL

Step	Action	The Facing the Challenge unit
1.	Select a topic that lends itself to multiple lines of inquiry including SRL.	The Facing the Challenge unit has multiple lines of inquiry (from Australian Curriculum): • **Reading and writing** (e.g. researching and writing biographies of famous individuals who have overcome challenges) • **General capabilities** (e.g. SRL)
2.	Incorporate lessons that explicitly teach SRL concepts.	The Facing the Challenge unit incorporates multiple lessons that focus on neuroplasticity and how engaging in challenging activities creates new neural pathways. This includes guest speakers (e.g. a neuroscientist) who extend students' understanding of neuroplasticity, and case studies where people's brains have changed when challenged.
3.	Deconstruct case studies.	The Facing the Challenge unit includes videos of people experiencing challenge (e.g. a person about to drop in to a high skateboard ramp) and discussion of what the person is experiencing and what might be effective and ineffective forms of self-talk. For example: • What sorts of things could this person be saying to themselves? • What might be helpful? • What might be unhelpful?

Step	Action	The Facing the Challenge unit
4.	Explicitly teach SRL strategies within the unit.	The Facing the Challenge unit explicitly teaches four SRL strategies (explored in detail in Table 19).
5.	Invite students to choose a personal challenge to work, documenting their progress as they go.	The Facing the Challenge unit requires every student to engage in a challenge for four weeks and create a video sharing their reflections about what strategies they used and what were most important for their given challenge context.
6.	Showcase learning journeys.	The Facing the Challenge unit includes an exhibition of learning where parents and other guests come to view the students' work, allowing students to celebrate their learning progress.

Table 19 shows that the 'Facing the Challenge' unit combines various learning activities to encourage SRL. An important part of this unit, as shown in Table 19, is the explicit teaching of four specific SRL strategies aimed at enhancing persistence and overcoming challenges.

Table 19. SRL strategies to overcome challenges

Strategy name	Description of strategy	Desired outcome
Repetition with modification	Repeated practise, but with minor pivots each time. In other words, you have to keep going at things and reflect on what you could do better each time.	Deliberate practise that leads to improved performance. Learners believe that they have to persevere to reap the rewards.
	To explain this strategy and highlight the importance of feedback and instructional self-talk, Rory uses a video about Austin's Butterfly: youtube.com/watch?v=E_6PskE3zfQ	Connection to neuroplasticity – for connections between synapses to be strengthened, new learning must be repeated. With repetition comes a reduction in the challenge posed by the learning.

Strategy name	Description of strategy	Desired outcome
Breaking a challenge into smaller parts	A metacognitive planning strategy: what do you have to do? What would be logical to do first? Which will be the most difficult parts? How could you overcome that difficulty?	Encourages planning and strategic thinking on how to do something at a more granular level. Focusing on a smaller, simpler aspect of a task increases the likelihood of success and progress, increasing confidence, motivation and self-efficacy.
Coach not a critic	Rory explains this as 'Coaches help you by giving you instructions and they help to keep your spirits high, and they don't criticise you because that's not very helpful.'	Reframe negative self-talk with supportive mastery-focused instructional self-talk. Doing so displays resilience and models a growth mindset. Often negative self-talk can be quite 'fixed' in nature, e.g. 'You're just not good at this.'
What's my *why*?	A strategy to help students focus on the value of the learning experience, rather than simply doing it to achieve a grade. Value could include the importance of doing hard things and the personal growth that comes from that. Maybe they are trying hard to improve at something in relation to a bigger goal such as improving in a sport or starting a specific career. By increasing the value, students become more motivated by the benefits that they see, why they're engaging in the challenge and why it's important to do hard things.	Increases task value and helps maintain effort. When a task gets difficult, thinking about the value of a task boosts motivation. This process involves a student recognising that the difficulty of the task is causing a decrease in effort, and potentially triggering negative emotions. Subsequently, the student should select a strategy to counteract this. A useful approach is to ask 'What's my *why*?' which helps to refocus on the task's value and enhance motivation.

ADAPTED FROM RORY MCCAUGHEY'S 'FACING THE CHALLENGE' UNIT.

The four strategies listed in Table 19 are brought to life in Rory's classroom through the use of 'strategy boxes' to help students engage with and understand the strategies in a tangible way. Refer Figure 12.

Figure 12. Examples of strategy boxes to support students' SRL

1
What's my *why*?
Ask 'What's my *why*?' Thinking about why a task is valuable or important to you motivates you to keep going!
• Why is the challenge important to complete or overcome? • Why is it valuable to you? How will it improve you as a person? • Are the skills or knowledge from the task going to be useful for you later in life?

2
Be a coach, not a critic
When giving yourself instructions it's important to be a coach, not a critic.
• Focus on taking the next step. 'Okay, the next thing I can try is …' • Create a reward for yourself for achieving a mini goal. 'Once I have made five baskets in a row, I will take a break and eat a snack.' • Suggest a small way to make an improvement. 'That last stitch was crooked and loose, next time I will tighten the wool more.' • Be supportive. 'You're trying hard and have made some good progress. Even though it's not perfect, you're doing well.'

FROM RORY MCCAUGHEY'S 'FACING THE CHALLENGE' UNIT, INCLUDED WITH PERMISSION.

These strategy boxes provide a hands-on approach to exploring and applying the strategies, making them more accessible and practical for students. In addition to the strategy boxes, one of Rory's colleagues also created a strategies poster as an anchor chart that could be displayed in the classroom; refer Figure 13.

Figure 13. Strategies poster from the 'Facing the Challenge' unit (included with permission)

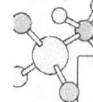

STRATEGIES FOR CHALLENGE

Introduction
Use this 'Strategies Pinboard' to select strategies to help when you feel challenged by your project. You can use one at a time, or multiple at the same time. Certain strategies might be more useful than others depending on the challenge.

Positive Self Talk

What's my why?
Why is this challenge important to you? What's the value? Why is it beneficial?

Be a coach, not a critic
Give yourself instructions

Repetition

Repeated efforts with modification.
What works?
What doesn't?
Trial and error.

Ask for advice from an expert

Ask an adult, expert or knowledgeable friend you know to give you tips!

Break it into smaller parts

Lots of challenges can seem big to begin with. Break the task into smaller parts and get started on one.

In addition to the strategies highlighted in the 'Facing the Challenge' unit, Rory also incorporated other techniques (though they were not the central focus) – including goal-setting strategies, both in terms of desired outcomes and the processes to achieve them, as well as a weekly planning strategy. This planning aspect enabled students to develop a clear, structured plan for their weekly activities.

To monitor and reinforce the application of these strategies, Rory and his team implemented a reflective practice at the end of each week. Students were invited to complete a seven-question reflection, which is detailed in Figure 14. This reflective exercise was designed to encourage students to critically assess their use of the strategies, understand their effectiveness and identify areas for improvement.

Figure 14. Reflective exercise

Written reflection
What was your goal for this week? Did you achieve it? Why or why not?
What's one thing that went particularly well? Why?
Did you face any specific challenges, obstacles or difficulties?
What strategies did you use to overcome the challenges or difficulties? Explain.
Did you use your time well? How do you know this?
What are you aiming to do better next week?
What learning from this week can you take away and use somewhere else? Another subject? A hobby? Another goal?

FROM RORY MCCAUGHEY'S 'FACING THE CHALLENGE' UNIT, INCLUDED WITH PERMISSION.

Students were prompted to reflect on various aspects of their learning each week: they identified what aspects went well and the reasons for this success, what didn't go as planned and why, and the specific strategies they employed and their effectiveness. The final question in every reflection session was consistently framed ('What learning from this week can you take away and use somewhere else?'), which was purposely designed to foster the ability to transfer learning across different subjects. Rory's role in this reflective process was pivotal. He provided targeted feedback on the students' reflections, focusing on their self-reported strategy use. This feedback was instrumental in enhancing the students' ability to effectively apply and adapt the strategies, thereby building their capacity for SRL and strategy application in various contexts.

Incorporate SRL strategy instruction into feedback conversations

Feedback also plays an important role in fostering students' SRL. The impact of feedback on learning is well established (e.g., William, 2017; William & Leahy, 2015). According to Hattie and Timperley (2007), effective feedback should feed up, back and forward in that it should give information about goals (up), information about the gap between current performance and goals (back) and offer steps to progress towards the goals (forward). Bellhäuser, Dignath and Theobald (2023), in their longitudinal field experiment exploring how feedback enhances college students' SRL, reported that confirmative (affirming students in their study approach) and transformative (explicitly teaching students strategies to progress learning) had the greatest impact on learners. When this combined thinking is applied to SRL, feedback should:

- support students' goals for SRL (up),
- provide information about the gap between current SRL performance and desired SRL performance (back/confirmative), and
- provide knowledge and strategies that enable the student to progress their SRL capabilities (forward/transformative).

Students often focus only on the final result when they receive feedback. This limits how much they engage with the feedback and reduces the chance that they will adjust their learning methods in the future. To counteract this concern, Dipesh Vadher (King David School, Vic) uses **triple impact**

feedback (three tiers of feedback, and engagement with that feedback) to help students to reflect on both learning product and process:

- **Level 1. Provide initial feedback:** First, when checking a student's work, Dipesh indicates a segment of their writing (e.g. a learning journal entry) or their response to a question that requires attention. Dipesh uses a pink pen to illuminate areas for students to think about, which his students fondly know as 'think pink'. These marked segments sometimes include comments but are often left without explicit guidance, prompting students to engage in self-reflection.

- **Level 2. Student responds to feedback:** Dipesh then provides students time in class to respond to the feedback in a green box, which the students fondly know as 'go green'. Figure 15 (overleaf) demonstrates Dipesh's 'think pink – go green' approach. Unfortunately, as this book is in black and white, I have annotated the image to indicate the 'think pink' and 'go green' sections, and included a colour version on my website: **shyambarr.com/book**.

- **Level 3. Teacher-student conversation:** In one-to-one discussions, Dipesh explores the strategies the student uses for SRL and offers explicit guidance on more effective strategies.

Dipesh has found the triple impact feedback approach to be highly effective for supporting student's SRL strategies. For example, one of Dipesh's Year 11 Chemistry students was struggling with problem-solving. The triple impact feedback approach led to a realisation on both parts (learner and teacher) that there were issues in how the student was taking notes and then trying to retrieve and access them. The unpacking of strategies around recording and organising information led to the student adopting a new approach to note-taking, and effective application led to improved performance in Chemistry.

Rory's and Dipesh's approaches highlight the integration of SRL strategy instruction into their teaching methods (Rory in the context of reading and writing; Dipesh in the context of Chemistry). It's important to remember that SRL, like any form of learning, is highly contextual and that students need to see relevance between taught strategies and their subject contexts.

Figure 15. A student work sample indicating the first two levels (think pink – go green) of Dipesh's triple impact feedback approach

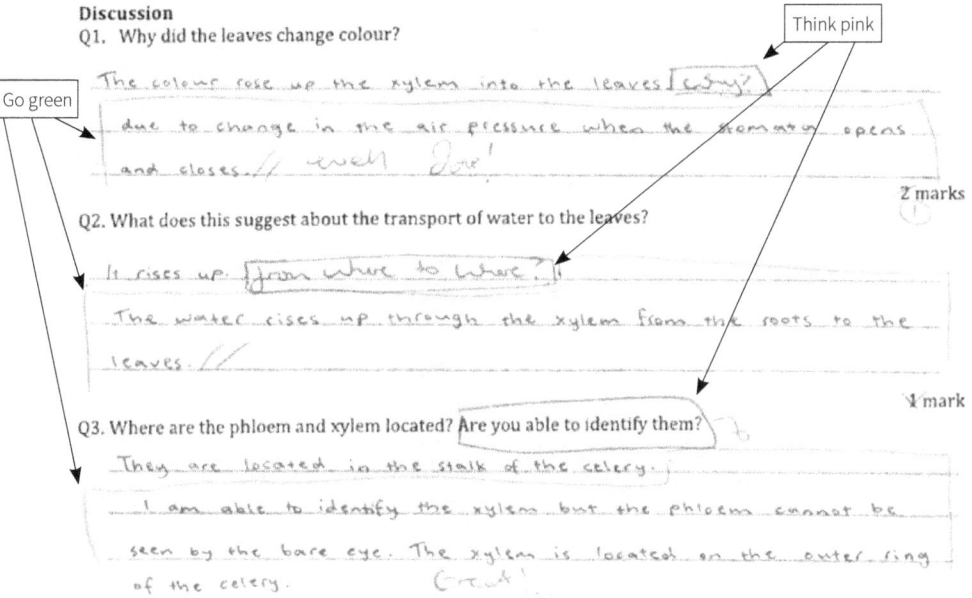

Offer a course in SRL

Researchers have also suggested that schools would benefit from including a specific subject stream to explore concepts of SRL with students (Vosniadou et al., 2021). There are many ways to create a course in any subject area, including SRL, and this involves several steps and considerations. Refer Table 20.

Table 20. Steps to develop a course in SRL

Step	Prompts
Establish target audience	• Who will be the focus of the SRL course? • Will this be a whole-school experience, a year level or a more targeted group? • Will this course be mapped over multiple year levels or a standalone program that exists in a single year level?

Step	Prompts
Clearly define the course objectives	• What are the learning intentions? • What are the success criteria? For example, students understand the principles of SRL, can implement SRL strategies in their learning, and regularly evaluate the effectiveness of these strategies.
Develop a scope and sequence and develop content	• What SRL models and concepts do students wish to learn about? • What strategies will the course focus on (e.g., goal-setting, time-management, self-assessment, reflection)? • Can you introduce digital tools to support SRL? There are examples of scope and sequences publicly available that offer a useful starting point. For example, if you visit the Victoria Curriculum and Assessment Authority website (https://victoriancurriculum.vcaa.vic.edu.au), you can click on Critical and Creative Thinking and generate a scope and sequence for metacognitive skills from Years 3–10.
Consider assessment and feedback approach	Include formative assessments to help students gauge their understanding and apply concepts in their learning. Provide constructive feedback to facilitate continuous improvement. This might be feedback on written reflections like Rory did in the 'Facing the Challenge' unit, or a triple impact feedback approach like Dipesh used.
Consider practical application	Learners could design strategic study plans incorporating SRL strategies and receive feedback on these plans.
Consider interactive and reflective learning	The course should be interactive. Use case studies, discussions and group activities to foster collaboration and deepen understanding. Encourage reflective practice whereby you analyse your teaching methods and consider how to incorporate SRL.
Other considerations	• Ensure the course caters to different learning preferences. • Offer flexibility in course pacing to model SRL principles. • Provide ample resources and support for teachers implementing SRL in their classrooms. • A dedicated teaching team? • What will the subject/course be called? • When will it launch and run?

Let's consider a couple of course examples. In 2017, as part of its then new Senior Years (9–12) Program, Melbourne Girls Grammar implemented a two-week student SRL course for Year 9 students. The course was a series of online modules and a workbook titled 'The Blueprint for Success', covering key motivational, cognitive, metacognitive and resource management concepts and strategies.

In 2024, Seymour College is dedicating two lessons per week to the explicit teaching of SRL strategies during Years 7 and 8. This includes students being explicitly taught about how the brain functions when learning, and exploration of key capabilities and different strategies that can be applied in different learning contexts.

Radford College has built the teaching of SRL strategies into Year 9 and 10 study skills courses – one period per cycle. In 2024, a greater SRL focus will be incorporated into Year 7 to 11 courses including the Year 7 transition program, Year 8 to 10 study skills courses and the Year 11 transition to senior school course.

These examples highlight a growing trend in schools recognising and prioritising the teaching of SRL strategies, and demonstrating a commitment to preparing students for effective learning and academic success. However, one of the challenges with a standalone SRL course is the potential lack of contextual application, as students often struggle to transfer knowledge across different subjects. To address this and maximise the effectiveness of SRL instruction, I suggest the following strategies in program design:

- **Involve subject teachers in SRL instruction:** Assign a teacher from each subject area to participate in teaching the SRL course. These teachers can then relay relevant concepts and strategies back to their respective teaching teams, ensuring that SRL is consistently reinforced across different subjects.
- **Align SRL course with subject curricula:** Develop a scope and sequence for the SRL course that mirrors those in other subjects. This parallel structure will help integrate SRL concepts directly into subject-specific learning.
- **Integrate SRL into lesson planning:** Create prompts for lesson planning that encourage teachers to incorporate SRL strategies into their classes. For example, if metacognitive self-talk strategies are taught in the SRL course, include a planning prompt about self-talk that is relevant to each specific subject.

- **Foster a whole-school approach to SRL:** As we'll discuss in Chapter 11, we can also develop a school-wide understanding of and appreciation for SRL. This holistic approach ensures that SRL is not seen as an isolated subject but as a fundamental aspect of the entire educational experience.

Move from study skills training to SRL training.

It's important to recognise that a course about study skills is not the same as a course about SRL. For example, Theobald (2021) found that study skill training that focuses on cognitive strategies (e.g. explanations about reading strategies, note-taking, test preparation) is less effective (effect size of 0.28) than 'metacognitive training' (0.63). In metacognitive training, students learn about metacognitive strategies that span the three phases of planning, monitoring and evaluating. Additionally, students are engaged in metacognitive reflection activities to help them develop greater awareness of themselves as learners and their learning processes, something that rarely occurs in study skills training programs. Therefore, courses about SRL exceed typical study skills programs in schools, by extending the focus from merely cognitive, to metacognitive, motivational, emotional and resource management.

Chapter summary

This chapter highlighted the transformative impact of incorporating SRL concepts and strategies into educational units. When you integrate an explicit focus on SRL concepts and strategies into a unit, a significant shift occurs in students' learning behaviours. They begin to build and expand their own set of SRL strategies, and, through consistent practise, notable advancements in their ability to apply these strategies in context become evident. Moreover, by providing targeted, strategy-focused feedback, you guide your students towards becoming more proficient self-regulated learners. And, by developing a dedicated course on SRL, there's an opportunity to extend these benefits beyond the confines of individual classroom interactions.

Take action

- Incorporate a learning intention and success criteria for SRL in your lessons. This is not necessarily teaching a new strategy each lesson, but rather sustaining a focus on SRL throughout lesson (e.g. the learning intention could be related to self-talk for a whole unit).
- Integrate the explicit teaching of SRL concepts and strategies into a unit of work.
- Implement a triple impact feedback approach that feeds forward and is transformative in helping students develop their repertoire of SRL strategies.
- Design a course about SRL that incorporates transfer elements.

Delve deeper

My website **shyambarr.com/book** includes links to the following resources so you can explore the concepts in this chapter further.

- ☐ Listen to the *Educate to Self-Regulate* podcast episode 8 where Rory and I discuss the 'Facing the Challenge' unit.
- ☐ Listen to the *Educate to Self-Regulate* podcast episode 20 where Dipesh and I discuss the triple impact feedback approach.
- ☐ Revisit Vosniadou et al.'s (2021) 'Teaching students how to learn: Setting the stage for lifelong learning'. Read section 3, pages 26–28.

Implementation intentions

Setting implementation intentions is a goal-setting strategy that involves writing down a specific plan of action with the when, where and how of accomplishing a task. This method is powerful because it moves beyond the realm of abstract goals into concrete plans. By doing so, it can significantly reduce mind-wandering and increase the chances of following through on behaviours that lead to success in learning and teaching.

To set implementation intentions, define a clear, actionable step that aligns with your learning or teaching goals.

Use the sentence structure: 'I will [action] at [time] on [day]' to articulate your intention. For example, 'I will share with my students the "living room of the mind" metaphor on Tuesday morning at 11am.'

Applying the strategy in the classroom

- Encourage students to identify specific actions they can take to improve their study habits.
- Provide time in class for students to write down their intentions.
- Discuss the importance of committing to these intentions and following up on progress.

Transfer to other contexts

Think about how implementation intentions could be used for personal development, workplace productivity or even in maintaining social relationships. Can committing to specific actions help in achieving broader life goals?

6
Pedagogies to enhance metacognition for SRL

Children must be taught how to think, not what to think.

— Margaret Mead

As explained in Chapter 2, metacognition is not only thinking about thinking, but also regulating that thinking. Remember the 'living room of the mind' metaphor? It's not only noticing what's on the TV, but having the remote to change that thinking. Activating metacognition requires us to empower students to actively engage in the metacognitive process of planning, monitoring and evaluating learning. To help students become self-regulated learners, you can activate their metacognition by modelling it yourself, and prompting students in each phase of planning, monitoring and evaluating.

In this chapter, I invite you to:

- explicitly model metacognition
- explicitly prompt metacognition using learning protocols to stimulate metacognitive reflection
- use a questioning framework that follows a progression of learning skills.

Explicitly model metacognition

You can model metacognition by thinking-aloud (as per the think-aloud protocols discussed in Chapter 3) as you engage in a learning task - demonstrating how you reflect on and manage your own learning. For many of us, thinking-aloud might be common practice, but there are nuances in the way we think aloud when explicitly focused on developing SRL. For examples of how to think-aloud and model metacognition for SRL, refer Table 21.

Table 21. Examples of how to explicitly model metacognition

Approach	Description
Explicitly demonstrate	Select a task relevant to the lesson – be it solving a maths problem, analysing a text or formulating a hypothesis in a science experiment. As you work through the task, speak out loud, describing each step of your thinking process. Articulate your understanding of the problem, hypothesise possible solutions and reason through your choices.
	For instance, while solving a maths problem on the board, you might say, 'First, I identify what is being asked. I then consider what information I have and what formulas might apply. I'm checking my understanding as I go to make sure each step makes sense.'
Articulate confusion and uncertainty	In moments of confusion or uncertainty, you might say, 'I'm not sure why this result came up, so I'm going to recheck my calculations,' or, 'This part of the text is ambiguous; let's explore it further.'
	If you, like many of us, find it difficult to show the students your fallibility, try framing up the notion of 'making mistakes' at the start of a task or a unit. E.g. 'It's likely that during this task I will get stuck or make a mistake, but I will talk this through as a method to progress towards a solution.'
Reflect on decisions	After making a decision, reflect on it out loud. For instance, if you choose a specific method to solve a complex problem, share with the class by saying, 'I opted for this strategy because it aligns with our topic last week on quadratic equations. Reflecting on it, I see that it simplified our problem-solving process because it broke down the steps clearly. However, I realise it may not have been the most time-efficient method. Next time, I might explore a different technique to compare effectiveness. This way, we can learn which methods are best suited to certain types of problems.'

Approach	Description
Connect to prior knowledge	Model how to connect new information to what you already know. 'This concept reminds me of …' or 'This is similar to what we learned last week when we …'
Use metacognitive language	Incorporating metacognitive language into everyday classroom dialogue can normalise the process of thinking about thinking. Phrases such as 'I am wondering …', 'I realised that …' or 'I decided to change …' highlight the ongoing reflective process.

Implementing the approaches from Table 21 allows you to think-aloud as you explicitly demonstrate how to work through a particular problem. You might pause when you experience challenge in the problem and express your feelings and uncertainty. As you verbalise your next steps, you might reflect out loud on the effectiveness of the decision or connect what you're learning to prior knowledge. The goal here is to make your internal process for thinking transparent to your students, so that it demystifies complex cognitive processes and makes your strategies transparent.

Eventually, as we explored in Chapter 3, you can encourage students to participate in making their thinking transparent by also thinking-aloud. This can be done in a whole-class setting or in small groups, where students articulate their thought processes to peers. It is important to note that some students may not be accustomed to reflecting on their learning processes, and some may find it difficult to articulate their thoughts. You can address these challenges by regularly modelling your own metacognitive learning processes and inviting students to share and discuss their reflections on their learning processes with the others in the class (in pairs, small groups or the whole class). You can also facilitate this process using metacognitive prompts to help students to be more reflective and strategic in their learning.

Explicitly prompt metacognition

Metacognitive prompts are strategic questions that teachers and learners use to encourage thinking about learning. They can be thought of in the three phases of SRL, as shown in Table 22.

Table 22. Metacognitive prompts for learning

Planning	Monitoring	Evaluating
• Have I seen a task like this before? • What kind of problem is this? • Have I seen similar problems before? • Do I need to have more information before I am able to solve this problem? • What prior knowledge do I have that might help? • What is my plan/goal for solving this problem? • What strategies will I use? • What resources will I need? • How will I stay focused and motivated during the task? • Are there any bits that I might find tricky? • What will I do if I get stuck?	• How am I staying focused and sticking to the plan? • Am I sure about what I am doing? • What are the things I do not understand? • Is the strategy that I have chosen working or do I need to try something else? • Do I need to try a different approach? • Have I used any strategies in the past that might help me here? • Do I have everything I need? • Could I check in with another student to see how I am progressing? • Have I revisited the instructions or rubric to see how I am going?	• Did I achieve my goal? • How did my plan help? Did I have to adapt it? • Have I mastered what I set out to learn? • What are the most important points? • What are the strategies that I used? • What are the strategies that worked well that I should remember for next time? • What do I need to do differently next time? • What have I learned about myself and my learning? • Did I stay motivated and on-task? What helped? • Do I need more/less support next time?

ADAPTED FROM SINS AND COLLEAGUES (2019; 2023), VOSNIADOU ET AL. (2021) AND EVIDENCE FOR LEARNING (N.D.).

Table 22 presents a series of questions designed to foster students' SRL in each of the three phases of SRL. I have phrased the questions in first person ('I' statements), as the goal for SRL is that these questions become internalised as part of a student's self-talk about learning. However, depending on the SRL competence of your learners, these questions can also be used by the educator to prompt a learner.

For example, during the planning phase, you might ask students questions to help them think about how they will approach the task – for example, 'What is your plan for tackling this assignment?' or 'What strategies will you use to understand these concepts?'. Questions in this phase prepare students to approach their work methodically. They encourage students to consider their prior knowledge, set clear goals, choose appropriate strategies, determine the resources they will need and anticipate potential challenges.

In the monitoring phase, as students progress with the task, you might ask them to consider, 'How are you doing with your plan?' or 'Which parts of this task are clear, and which are confusing?', encouraging a level of monitoring and self-assessment that might lead to a strategy adjustment. This set of questions prompts students to actively reflect on their progress while engaged in the task. They are encouraged to assess the effectiveness of their strategies, utilise past experiences to overcome current challenges and ensure they have the necessary resources. The questions also suggest peer interaction to evaluate their ongoing performance.

Lastly, after students complete a task or learning activity, you might ask, 'What worked well for you in this activity?' or 'What would you do differently next time?'. This helps students to think critically about their learning process and outcomes. In this final phase, students assess their performance against their initial goals. They reflect on the effectiveness of their planning and strategies, their motivation levels and the need for future support. This phase culminates in self-reflection on learning and personal growth.

In the classroom, these questions can be used as prompts for individual reflection, group discussion, or as a structured guide for written self-evaluations. They can be integrated into various stages of learning activities across all subjects to help students become more aware of their learning processes, ultimately promoting SRL. They encourage active engagement with learning material, promote higher-order thinking skills and help students become more independent in their learning. Additionally, metacognitive prompts can aid you in understanding your students' learning processes, which can inform instructional decisions. For example, you might ask a student 'What is your goal?' and this immediately prompts the student to reflect on what they are trying to achieve in a particular learning task.

Metacognitive prompts are extremely versatile and can also be integrated into lessons as learning protocols.

Using learning protocols that stimulate metacognitive reflection

To enhance SRL, you can implement a structured learning protocol specifically designed to stimulate metacognitive reflection. Such a protocol involves a series of questions that prompts learners to think about their own learning process, strategies and challenges before, during and after a task. For example, refer Figure 16.

Figure 16. SRL learning protocol

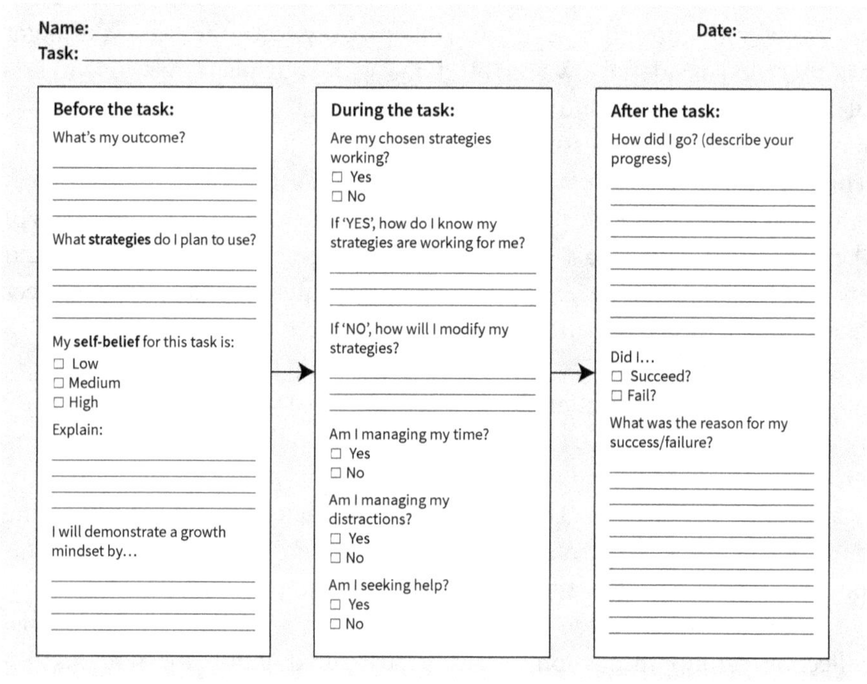

Name: _____   Date: _____
Task: _____

Before the task:

What's my outcome?
_____
_____
_____

What **strategies** do I plan to use?
_____
_____
_____

My **self-belief** for this task is:
☐ Low
☐ Medium
☐ High

Explain:
_____
_____

I will demonstrate a growth mindset by…
_____
_____
_____

During the task:

Are my chosen strategies working?
☐ Yes
☐ No

If 'YES', how do I know my strategies are working for me?
_____
_____

If 'NO', how will I modify my strategies?
_____
_____

Am I managing my time?
☐ Yes
☐ No

Am I managing my distractions?
☐ Yes
☐ No

Am I seeking help?
☐ Yes
☐ No

After the task:

How did I go? (describe your progress)
_____
_____
_____
_____

Did I…
☐ Succeed?
☐ Fail?

What was the reason for my success/failure?
_____
_____
_____
_____

BARR, 2020.

Note: The word 'fail' was normalised in the classroom setting in which the protocol was used. If you find it affronting, then please remove or replace with an alternative word. However, normalising failure as a common part of a learning process is valuable for a lifelong approach to learning.

The SRL learning protocol (Figure 16) consists of three sections: before the task, during the task and after the task. The 'before the task' section is designed to be completed at the beginning of a task (after the student understands the task requirements and has analysed the task); the 'during the task' section is designed to be completed midway through the task, and requires the teacher to stop the class and direct completion; while the 'after the task' section is designed to be filled out following task completion. This mirrors the phases of SRL: planning, monitoring and evaluating. You might introduce the protocol by discussing concepts related to self-efficacy (i.e.

the students' self-belief that they can execute the required behaviours to be successful) or help-seeking (i.e. the strategies a student might engage if they require help). Additionally, as students engage in the protocol, they develop their goal-setting and strategy selection.

Other examples included below are adapted from Eilam and Reiter (2014); refer Figure 17 and Figure 18.

The learning plan and evaluation (Figure 17) was adapted from Eilam and Reiter (2014). The original tool has been successfully utilised in studies within a science context for enhancing students' time management and self-regulation skills over a full academic year. This instrument, detailed in a straightforward form, allows students to track their learning progress weekly. Essentially, students set distinct goals for each week, such as specific topics. With 22 lines representing each week, it includes columns for the date, teacher's suggested plan, students' actual learning and the gap between these. It prompts students to reflect on reasons for any discrepancies, propose actions to bridge gaps and evaluate their weekly performance.

The weekly plan and evaluation (Figure 18), also adapted from Eilam and Reiter (2014), is tailored for closer monitoring of progress during each specific session in a week. It consists of four main parts: goal-setting, planning and reality columns, and reflection and self-evaluation. At the start of each lesson, students set specific short-term goals, either based on the teacher's suggestions, the textbook or their own understanding. This helps them focus on manageable goals for each session. In the planning column, they outline detailed activities such as answering textbook questions, summarising content or creating concept maps. These activities are sequenced and time-allocated to achieve the stated goals. Students assess their plans with questions such as, 'Will this plan achieve the weekly goals?', and rate their confidence in executing the plan. As students enact their plans, they record the types of activities and the time spent on each in the reality column. This process enables them to identify any discrepancies between planned and actual activities, making necessary adjustments. The reflection empowers students to reflect on the gap and bring awareness to patterns in behaviour that hinder them from reading their goals and planned actions.

Figure 17. Learning plan and evaluation

Week beginning	Plan	Reality	Gap	Reason for gap	Plan to rectify gap
Mon 11/3	Topic 1.1 Read Chapter 1 of the textbook, take notes and complete the practice questions at the end of the chapter on Topic 1.1.	Read half of Chapter 1, took some notes, but didn't get to the practice questions.	Chapter wasn't fully read, and practice questions were not attempted.	I underestimated the time it would take to read the chapter and take detailed notes. Also, I had an unexpected family commitment on Wednesday evening.	I will schedule two additional 30-minute study sessions on Tuesday and Thursday next week to finish reading Chapter 1 and to work on the practice questions. I'll also review my time management for the week to ensure I allocate enough time for studying.
Mon 18/3	Topic 1.2				
Mon 25/3	Topic 1.3				
Mon 1/4	Topic 1.4				
...					

ADAPTED FROM EILAM & REITER (2014, P. 717) – YEARLY SELF-REPORT INSTRUMENT.

Figure 18. Weekly plan and evaluation

Learning goal: _____ Date: _____

Day/time	Plan		Reality		Reflection on performance	
	Activity	Time allocated	Activity	Time spent	Is there a gap?	Where is the gap? (e.g. time, activity, order of tasks)
Monday	Draft introduction for English essay	40 minutes (or 11–11:40am)	Wrote first paragraph of intro	30 minutes	Yes	I had to respond to email from English teacher and re-read task instructions
...						
...						
...						

Reflection:

What patterns have emerged in the gap between my planning and execution (reality)?
What strategies might help me minimise the gap?
What tasks are still to be completed?

ADAPTED FROM EILAM & REITER (2014, P. 718) – YEARLY SELF-REPORT INSTRUMENT.

The learning protocols documented in Figures 16, 17 and 18 support students in reflecting on their learning, identifying any gaps and understanding the causes of these gaps. If you're concerned about the time commitment involved in teaching and filling out these forms, remember that teaching any new protocol will take time in the first instance; however, as students become familiar with the process, completing a simple learning protocol can be done within a few minutes as students settle in at the beginning of a lesson. To mitigate a large time investment at the start, consider choosing a section of a protocol to focus on as a scaffolded approach to using the protocol.

Use a questioning framework that follows a progression of learning skills

Employing a questioning framework that supports students in developing a language of learning can also enhance their SRL. For example, a learning and responding matrix (ALARM) is an explicit questioning framework that follows a progression of learning skills (Woods, 2009). It is founded on the principle that to become an effective self-regulated learner, students must ask the right question, at the right time and at the right depth. ALARM offers a progression of learning skills and associated questions; refer Table 23.

Table 23. ALARM progression of learning skills

ALARM progression of learning skills	Description	Example questions and instructions
Name and define	Identify and define key areas related to the topic of inquiry.	• What are the areas, components/parts, steps and stages within the process/task/topic of inquiry itself?
Describe	Describe features, characteristics or aspects of each area in more detail.	• What are the characteristics of each of the components under consideration? • Outline the details of a particular topical program. What does each part look like? • What are relevant examples that demonstrate/illustrate an idea or parts of the process?

ALARM progression of learning skills	Description	Example questions and instructions
Explain significance	Explain the purpose, function, role or importance of the areas or features described. Consider the cause and/or impact/effect.	• Why is this important? • What problem is each addressing or attending to? • What is each part/feature trying to achieve? • What is the aim? What is each part's effect – what's the reason behind it and what is the impact?
Analyse	Understand how the areas, features or characteristics work to achieve their purpose or the effect. Further to this, attempt to discover how they work together or relate to each other and the relationship between the cause and effect.	• How is it working towards its intended or unintended effect/impact? • How is it achieving its cause? How do the causes/effects occur? • How are the parts related to each other and/or are interrelated, which may include comparison/contrast between them to understand their relationship to each other or to the process itself?
Moment of self-reflection and risk-taking		
Critically analyse	Consider the positives and/or negatives of the content/features, the strengths and/or weaknesses, biases and/or assumptions.	• What are the advantages and/or disadvantages? • How is it beneficial and/or harmful? • How are some or all features, characteristics or impacts more positive and/or negative than the others? • How/why do they compare/contrast positively and/or negatively?
Evaluate	Make judgements about the extent of the value and effectiveness of *each* area of the topic based on the critical analysis.	• To what extent does each area carry out its intended or unintended purpose or aim or goal? What is the value of the impact upon something or someone?

ALARM progression of learning skills	Description	Example questions and instructions
Critically evaluate	Consider a *broader* range of factors, implications, and consequences. This involves a nuanced overall judgement that assesses the value of the multiple areas within the topic.	• To what extent are some of the areas more effective/successful than others? • To what extent is the overall process itself effective/successful?
Conceptualise topic	Synthesise all the information and insights and skills gained to form new understandings, ideas or theories.	• Summarise or make an interpretation on the developmental process and its change of procedures over time. • Express why the interrelationship is important for the complete process.
Appreciate	Acknowledge the value of what has been learned to person and life.	• Why is it valuable to have learned this? • Why is what I've learned important to my life? • Why is understanding the topic concept important for life. Why should it be learned?

WOODS, 2009; INCLUDED WITH PERMISSION.

In the first column of Table 23 you can see that there are eight levels to the ALARM progression of learning skills. The progression of skills is divided by a moment of reflection (where a learner goes from gathering information to forming their stance about the information, i.e. from surface-level to deep learning), briefly described in the second column, with example questions and instructions listed in the third column.

I see two ways in which ALARM can be used to support students' SRL. Firstly, the ALARM progression of learning skills and associated questions can be used across the curriculum to support student engagement in different phases of SRL. For example, you might teach students about ALARM, including the progression of skills, to help students develop familiarity with

ALARM. As part of your teaching, you might use ALARM to metacognitively model or prompt your students through the different phases of SRL:

- 'Here I am *describing* ...'
- 'How are you progressing?'
- 'What do you notice about your current stage of engagement with this information?'
- 'What's your goal moving forward?'

However, the real power of ALARM for SRL lies in the students' understanding of the framework for questioning. Once a learner understands ALARM – that is, they have a familiarity with and acquisition of the progression of learning skills and the associated questioning – they can begin to internalise the questions as self-questions to help progress their learning. For instance, in the self-reflection phase of SRL, a learner can use the ALARM progression of learning skills to self-evaluate their progress and knowledge development (e.g. how does this piece of work achieve the *describe* progression?). Following this self-reflection and self-evaluation, in the forethought phase of SRL, a learner can use the ALARM progression of learning skills to set goals for constructing knowledge and understanding (e.g. where to next? What is the next stage in the progression of learning skills?).

Secondly, the ALARM progression of learning skills and questions can also be applied directly to the subject of SRL, the intention being to help students develop a deeper understanding of SRL concepts and strategies, and thus improve their engagement in SRL. When entering from this angle, the teacher can use ALARM to design learning and teaching activities to support students' development of SRL knowledge and skills – which will lead to greater students' SRL. Alternatively, students can use questions to form an inquiry into SRL (once again developing their knowledge and skills of SRL for themselves). Refer Table 24 (overleaf).

Table 24 shows that the ALARM progression of learning skills can be applied at the two levels of SRL knowledge, where a student is developing their conceptual knowledge about SRL and their knowledge about the strategies they use to regulate or change their learning.

Thus far, I have explained how ALARM, as an explicit questioning framework, can support SRL as a metacognitive prompt for learning in any subject, but also as a self-questioning strategy that can support learners' engagement in the planning, monitoring and evaluating of their learning. Alongside approaches such as ALARM, it's important to provide students with opportunities to deliberately practise their SRL.

Table 24. ALARM applied to the subject of SRL

ALARM progression of learning skills	Example questions in the context of SRL
Name and define	• What are the main components and corresponding strategies of SRL that I should know about? • Can I define what these parts mean? • Can I identify and define the learning strategies that I am currently aware of?
Describe	• What are the features/characteristics of each component and corresponding strategy? • Can I describe the learning strategies that I have used in recent tasks? • Can I describe what I currently do to study and manage my learning? • What specific study methods (such as making flashcards or writing summaries) am I using right now?
Explain significance	• What is the intended impact/effect of each strategy? • What does each SRL strategy aim to achieve? • Why are these learning strategies important or useful in my studies? • What is the outcome of engaging in SRL?

Analyse	• How are the different components of SRL related?
	• How do the different components work together to help me engage in more effective learning?
	• How do my different learning strategies (motivational, cognitive, metacognitive etc.) work together to help me achieve my academic goals?
	  – E.g. How do my planning strategies relate to the way I currently study and remember information?
	  – E.g. How do my choices about where and when to study interact with my planning strategies?

Moment of self-reflection and risk-taking	
Critically analyse	• What are the benefits and costs associated with engaging in SRL? • Can I see the positives of engaging in each stage of SRL? • Are there any ways I might be missing something in my approach or ways I could do better in how I self-regulate my learning? • What are the strengths and/or limitations of the learning strategies I use?

ALARM progression of learning skills	Example questions in the context of SRL

Evaluate	• To what extent are each of the ways I self-regulate my learning really working for me?
	• To what extent are my strategies assisting or not assisting me to meet my goals?
	• Based on my recent performance, how effective are each of my current learning strategies?
	• To what extent are my current learning strategies helping me achieve my learning objectives?
	  – E.g. To what extent am I good at figuring out when I understand something well or when I need to change each of my study tactics?
	  – E.g. What strategies help me learn best, and why?

Critically evaluate	• To what extent are some of the areas within SRL more effective for me than others? • To what extent is the overall process of engaging in SRL itself effective/successful? • Looking at how I've been learning, how do these SRL strategies help or not help me do well in learning the topics in school? • Reflecting on my overall approach to learning, to what extent do my strategies need to evolve or change for future learning challenges?
Conceptualise topic	• In its totality what is the main idea of SRL? • Thinking about everything I know about SRL, how might I change the way I self-regulate my learning in the future? • Thinking about the broad repertoire of SRL strategies, how can I adjust my SRL approach moving forward? • What new ideas or changes can I think of for how I might tackle learning in new or tough subjects?
Appreciate	• Why is it important to learn about SRL? • Why is it valuable to have learned about SRL? • Why is it important to be able to evaluate each of the components and strategies within SRL? • Why is it important to develop my SRL strategies? • How has my approach to learning changed this year? • How does the ability to use SRL enrich my learning experience? • How does developing my SRL knowledge and skills support me beyond school, and more broadly, throughout life?

Chapter summary

This chapter outlined the importance of metacognition in SRL, highlighting two key strategies: teachers modelling metacognitive skills and prompting students to reflect on their thinking. It detailed how you can demonstrate metacognition through verbalising your thought processes during different learning stages, and how structured questions can guide students to evaluate their learning strategies. Additionally, the chapter discussed learning protocols that allow students to monitor their progress and adjust their approaches, emphasising that teaching metacognition is about teaching students how to think about their learning, rather than what to think.

Take action

- Teach students a set of questions they can ask themselves to help them plan, monitor and evaluate their learning.
- Provide students with a set of metacognitive questions that can help them self-regulate during learning:
  - embedded within a task
  - prompted reflection during class/conversation
  - formal reflective protocols post-assessment/post-feedback.

Delve deeper

My website **shyambarr.com/book** includes links to the following resources so you can explore the concepts in this chapter further.

- [ ] Revisit Vosniadou et al (2021) 'Teaching students how to learn: Setting the stage for lifelong learning'. This time, read section 5, pages 34–37.
- [ ] Explore Evidence for Learning's modelling and questioning tools for metacognition and SRL.

SRL TOOLBOX

Self-evaluating self-efficacy

Self-evaluating our self-efficacy is a fundamental component in fostering SRL. When we assess our belief in our ability to teach SRL strategies or to execute a particular task, we generate awareness of our self-efficacy. With awareness, we can make better choices about how we engage with the task and the strategies that we select. This self-assessment prompts us to reflect on and refine our learning approach. Learners with high self-efficacy are more likely to persist through challenges, thereby modelling for students productive learning behaviours.

Take a moment to complete the following table:

SRL teaching activity	Confidence level (i.e. self-efficacy)				
	1. Not at all confident	2. A little confident	3. Somewhat confident	4. Very confident	5. Completely confident
a. Stimulating metacognitive reflection (e.g. 'think about how you learned this skill' or 'reflect on your learning process')					
b. Explicitly teaching SRL strategies using NEMO-T (name, explain, model, opportunity, transfer)					
c. Teaching motivational strategies (e.g. performance versus mastery goal-setting)					
d. Teaching cognitive strategies (e.g. attention focusing, retrieval practice)					
e. Teaching metacognitive strategies (e.g. self-talk, self-instructions, planning)					

SRL teaching activity	Confidence level (i.e. self-efficacy)				
	1. Not at all confident	2. A little confident	3. Somewhat confident	4. Very confident	5. Completely confident
f. Teaching resource management strategies (e.g. time-management, help-seeking)					
g. Teaching emotion regulation strategies (e.g. identifying triggers, breathing techniques)					
h. Clarifying the benefit of strategy use					
i. Activating transfer of strategy use					

Applying the strategy in the classroom

You can integrate self-evaluation of self-efficacy into your classroom by replacing the first column with actions required for a task specific for your subject (e.g. task-specific actions, general learning behaviours or a selection of SRL strategies). Then, model the completion of the table and explain the concept of self-efficacy (e.g. 'believing in your ability to complete a task directly affects your engagement and performance in the task'). Provide students with the new version of the self-efficacy table and have them rate their confidence in completing the different tasks. Make sure to incorporate regular check-ins where students can update their ratings and reflect on their progress. Encourage them to set personal goals based on their self-evaluations and to identify strategies that might help improve their confidence in areas where they feel less assured.

Transfer to other contexts

Consider a recent challenge or new skill you've encountered outside the classroom – perhaps in a hobby, sport or another subject area. Reflect on your initial confidence in addressing this challenge or learning this new skill. Now, using the self-efficacy table, rate your confidence in these areas again. Think about how the strategies you've learned in class can be applied to this new context. How can recognising and adjusting your self-efficacy influence your approach and success in various areas of your life?'

7
A positive classroom climate for SRL

*Students don't care how much you know,
until they know that you care.*

— John Maxwell

Alongside the explicit teaching of SRL concepts and strategies, and metacognitive prompting and modelling, it's imperative to consider how classroom climate influences SRL. Classroom climate refers to the overall atmosphere or environment within a classroom, which is influenced by factors such as teaching methods, student-teacher relationships, and the psychological and physical safety students perceive. A positive classroom climate is crucial for promoting students' SRL because it fosters an environment of trust and respect, which encourages students to take risks, engage in learning activities and develop their ability to learn independently. A supportive and inclusive classroom climate also helps students feel valued and understood, which boosts their motivation and confidence to manage their learning process effectively (Callan et al., 2020; 2022).

In this chapter, I invite you to:

- cultivate an SRL classroom
- enhance approaches that indirectly promote SRL:
    - incorporate opportunities for cooperative learning
    - create a constructivist learning environment

- provide students with autonomous learning experiences (e.g. self-direction)
- contextualise learning in real life (activate transfer).
- adjust teaching as students improve their SRL skills.

Cultivate an SRL classroom

When it comes to crafting an SRL classroom climate, there are a number of practices and characteristics of the classroom to be considered. Refer Table 25.

Table 25. Aspects of a classroom climate for SRL

Practice	Description
Fostering a collaborative learning environment	Cultivate a respectful and supportive atmosphere where students and teachers collaborate as partners in learning, establish routines and appreciate diverse participation. • Clear expectations. • Supportive relationships that enable academic risks and full engagement in learning. • Respectful and encouraging communication between teachers and students. • Familiar routines and varied valued participation structures. • Teachers and students co-construct knowledge, supporting student SRL.
Enhancing student autonomy	Empower students through explicit instruction in SRL skills, model these skills and encourage self-assessment, self-reflection and strategic decision-making. • Acknowledge students' perspectives and choices in their learning process. • Involve students in decision-making about what and how to learn. • Adjust tasks and environments to allow student control over challenge level.
Implementing instructional strategies for SRL	Implement instructional methods that include: • explicit teaching of SRL skills • formative, descriptive, task-specific feedback focused on the learning process • challenging tasks that promote strategic action • iterative learning activities that support goal-setting and adaptation (e.g. multiple drafts; long-term).

Practice	Description
Providing SRL support mechanisms	Develop classroom practices that prompt and support SRL. • Help-seeking strategies and frameworks. • Use cues, prompts or strategic questions to encourage SRL. • Engage students in metacognitive dialogue and reflection. • Opportunities for students to practise and apply SRL skills in various contexts. • Model SRL by thinking-aloud.
Encouraging peer-led learning and motivation	Encourage peer co-learning and provide motivational messages that connect effort with outcomes, facilitating a community of learners who support each other's growth. • Cooperative learning and peer evaluation support SRL. • Encourage students to attribute successes to SRL and efforts as opposed to ability.
Adapting to individual needs	Design and adapt learning activities and assessments to cater to individual differences, allowing all students to engage meaningfully and succeed. E.g. flexible tasks and assessments.

ADAPTED FROM CALLAN ET AL. (2020; 2022), DIGNATH ET AL. (2022) AND PERRY ET AL. (2020).

Table 25 highlights the importance of fostering strong student-teacher relationships, establishing clear routines and positioning all members as active learners. It highlights the necessity for teachers to serve as role models for SRL skills, provide effective feedback and facilitate connections between strategic actions and outcomes. Table 25 further suggests that prompting SRL, engaging students in iterative learning cycles and designing challenging tasks are pivotal for cultivating an environment conducive to self-regulation.

Enhance approaches that indirectly promote SRL

To craft a classroom climate supportive of SRL, you can also indirectly promote students' SRL (Dignath et al., 2022). We'll look at four approaches to do this.

Incorporate opportunities for cooperative learning

Incorporating cooperative learning into the classroom is essential in promoting SRL among students. This collaborative approach aligns with the notion that the learning environment significantly influences SRL, transitioning it into a socially engaged process. Through cooperative learning, students engage in co-regulation, where they collectively support each other to refine their learning strategies and negotiate shared goals and perceptions. This interaction not only enriches individual learning experiences but fosters a sense of community and shared responsibility, critical for developing self-regulation skills. By working in groups, students are exposed to varied perspectives and approaches, enhancing their problem-solving skills and academic resilience. Thus, cooperative learning acts as a scaffold, enabling students to internalise self-regulatory practices and eventually become independent, self-regulated learners. Table 26 provides a brief description of some approaches to supporting students' SRL through cooperative learning, along with a short description and classroom example for each:

Table 26. Examples of cooperative learning

Approach	Description	Classroom example
Jigsaw	Students are divided into small groups. Each member is given a unique piece of information to learn and then teach to their group members.	A history teacher divides the class into groups, assigning each student a different aspect of World War II to research and present to their group.
Jigsaw II	A variation of the original jigsaw. After initial group study, students are reorganised into expert groups to discuss their segment before returning to their original groups to teach what they've learned.	In a science class, students first study different ecosystems in separate groups, then meet in expert groups to deepen their understanding of each ecosystem before returning to teach their original group.
Reciprocal questioning	Students work in pairs or small groups to generate and answer questions about the material being learned, promoting deeper understanding.	In a literature class, students read a novel and then work in pairs, asking each other thought-provoking questions about the book's themes and characters.
Scripted cooperation	Students work in pairs with assigned roles (e.g. summariser, questioner) to ensure active participation and comprehension of the material.	During a maths lesson, one student solves a problem on the board while the other acts as a questioner, probing the reasoning behind each step.

Approach	Description	Classroom example
Student teams-achievement divisions	Students are placed in mixed-ability teams. They study instructional material together, and then individually complete quizzes, which contribute to the team's total score.	In a geography class, students work in teams to learn about different countries. Each student takes a quiz on the material, and their scores are combined to create a team score.

The approaches documented in Table 26 encourage active participation, collaborative learning and SRL.

Create a constructivist learning environment

Creating a constructivist learning environment is also a key strategy for fostering SRL in students. This educational approach places learners at the centre of the learning process, where they actively construct knowledge through critical thinking and problem-solving within real-world contexts. Such an environment nurtures SRL by prompting learners to integrate new information with their existing knowledge base, promoting deeper understanding and retention over mere memorisation. With the teacher acting as a facilitator, students are encouraged to explore, reflect and collaborate, which are vital components of self-regulation. This empowerment through personal discovery leads to a more meaningful and personalised learning experience, essential for developing autonomous and lifelong learners.

To foster a constructivist learning environment, consider incorporating activities such as:

- Beginning lessons by revisiting topics students are already familiar with, setting the stage for new information (i.e., activating prior knowledge).
- Guiding students in drawing connections between what they already know and the new concepts being introduced, aiding in the construction of a solid knowledge foundation.
- Embedding new information within contexts that are rich in meaning and relevance to the students' experiences.
- Sparking curiosity and cognitive engagement by presenting information that challenges existing understandings.

- Presenting problems that are complex and have multiple paths to resolution, encouraging creative and critical thinking.
- Motivating students to delve into research tasks that require problem-solving, hypothesis testing, and evidence-based argumentation.
- Adopting varied educational approaches, such as problem-based, project-based, and design thinking methodologies, to view learning through diverse lenses.

Provide students with autonomous learning experiences

Autonomous learning empowers learners to take charge of their educational journey, fostering self-direction and personal responsibility. This approach involves students setting their own learning goals, choosing resources and self-assessing their progress. It places a strong emphasis on critical thinking, problem-solving and the ability to independently seek and use resources. Importantly, autonomy in learning doesn't imply unrestricted freedom; rather, it operates within a structured framework that guides students' choices and actions. By enabling learners to explore topics of personal interest and relevance at their own pace, autonomous learning nurtures lifelong learning skills and motivates students to engage deeply with their education.

In 2023, educators Amelia Clay and Taleasha Bray at Bonython Primary School (ACT, Australia) introduced an innovative approach to self-directed learning called 'Smart Time'. For 20 minutes after lunch, students in their Years 5/6 class engaged in activities related to their personal SMART goals, which they had set earlier. This practice allowed students autonomy in choosing their focus, methods and collaboration partners. The initiative, fostering independent learning and goal-setting as key aspects of the planning phase of SRL, showed potential for expansion across multiple year levels due to its emphasis on personal inquiry. Amelia and Taleasha's implementation of 'Smart Time' reflects a progressive step in educational strategies, emphasising student autonomy and self-driven learning.

Other examples of autonomous learning include:

- personalised learning
- problem or project-based learning
- interdisciplinary learning.

Please note: providing students with autonomous learning experiences is a way to encourage the development of SRL skills. However, it's important to recognise that without the necessary foundational knowledge or abilities in SRL, students might find it challenging to navigate these experiences effectively. To facilitate a successful transition into autonomous learning, it's crucial to ensure that students have access to suitable support systems, such as transition programs, explicit strategy instruction and/or learning coaches. These resources can assist in building their SRL skills, either in preparation for or concurrently with their engagement in autonomous learning settings.

Contextualise learning in real life

Contextualising learning in real-life scenarios is vital for promoting effective learning and application skills. When learning is anchored in real-world contexts, it transcends mere academic exercises, becoming more meaningful and memorable. This approach, involving problem-solving with authentic tasks and reflective discussions, fosters the ability to activate and transfer knowledge to various situations. As learning is inherently tied to its acquisition context, providing diverse, realistic scenarios enhances students' adaptability and ability to apply what they've learned in structurally different settings. This method not only deepens understanding but also prepares students for practical application in their future endeavours.

To contextualise learning, you should integrate learning in a real-life context, ensuring learning applies to the real world. Illuminate the learning content in diverse contexts and/or in diverse ways of looking at a problem. The problems should be as realistic and authentic as possible.

Adjusting teaching as student SRL skills improve

As you create a classroom climate for SRL, you witness learners increasing their competence for SRL, allowing for greater autonomy and a fundamental shift in your role as a teacher from *directing* learning to *coaching* learning – an approach that focuses on guiding and supporting learners through personalised feedback and encouragement, fostering their ability to set goals, develop strategies and reflect on their own learning process. Figure 19 provides a visual representation of the process of change in teaching practice as your students increase their SRL competence and manage increasing levels of autonomy.

As depicted in Figure 19, during the initial phase of developing SRL competence the teacher's role is primarily to provide *direction* in SRL knowledge and tactics. As students make progress towards becoming adept self-regulated learners, the interaction between student and teacher evolves. Initially, it moves into a *consulting* phase, where the student and teacher jointly discuss strategies, yet the teacher is the one who ultimately guides the choice of strategy. The relationship then advances to a *partnership*, characterised by mutual discussion and joint decision-making on strategies. Finally, it culminates in a *coaching* phase, where discussions still occur, but the decision-making is largely in the hands of the student, showcasing their heightened SRL competence. Despite the student's increased autonomy, the teacher continues to play a significant role, which adapts according to the student's growing abilities. It's important to acknowledge that the starting point for these engagement levels may vary based on the individual student or class context. For instance, you might begin at the Direct level with certain students or classes, while starting at the Partner level with others.

Figure 19. The four levels of change towards creating a classroom climate for SRL

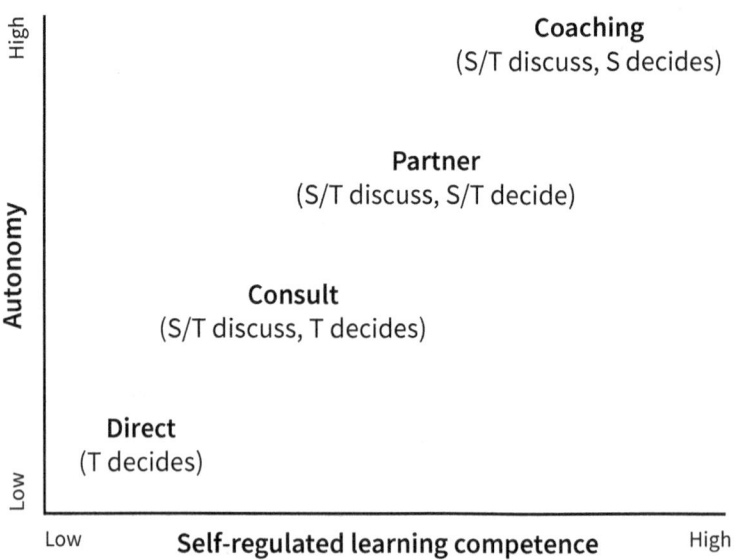

ADAPTED FROM THE INSTITUTE OF COACHING AND CONSULTING PSYCHOLOGY (2016).

Another way to think about the changes for students' SRL competence is through the lens of the conscious competence framework; refer Table 27.

Table 27. The conscious competence framework applied to SRL

	Unconscious incompetence: Learner is unaware of their lack of skill and proficiency	Conscious incompetence: Learner is aware of their lack of skill, but is not yet proficient	Conscious competence: Learner is able to use the skill but only with effort	Unconscious competence: Performing the skill becomes automatic
Behaviours	Unaware and unskilled learner. Not self-regulating as a learner (lacks knowledge and strategies).	Aware but unskilled learner. Aware of SRL and its importance but lacks knowledge of how to self-regulate their learning.	Aware, skilled learner. Applies skill in selected academic context or position.	Automated (allowing for deeper level of engagement with other aspects of learning) and transferred. Applies orientation, knowledge and skills to different domain.
Outcomes	Low achievement, lack of success, etc.	Metacognitive awareness (self-awareness).	Increased academic achievement and metacognitive control.	Excellent academic achievement. Automatised skill set – new normal.
Level of autonomy	Low autonomy.	Low autonomy.	Some opportunities for autonomy.	High autonomy.

Table 27 adapts the four stages of conscious competence to students' SRL competence. A student who is not self-regulating their learning very well is likely starting at the *unconscious incompetence* level. This learner is unaware of their learning processes and unskilled at self-regulating their learning. I'm noting here that SRL is a practice and that even a skilled self-regulated learner may, at times (depending on various factors) may appear as if operating at the *unconscious incompetence* level, so it is important to differentiate between those who demonstrate unconscious incompetence consistently (as a pattern) or just in a single moment. As you begin to create a culture for SRL, the student becomes increasingly aware of their learning processes and develops the skills to self-regulate those learning processes, moving them through *conscious incompetence* to *conscious competence* and *unconscious competence*. In this final stage the learner has wired in the identity of a learner, understands deeply their own learning processes and possesses a deep and broad repertoire of strategies that they can use to regulate their learning in different tasks, situations and domains.

Chapter summary

This chapter equipped you with the knowledge and tools to effectively craft an SRL classroom climate. It emphasised the benefit of incorporating four key pedagogies: cooperative learning, constructivist learning environments, autonomous learning experiences and real-life contextualisation of learning. You now realise that your teaching practice must evolve to adequately respond to your students' increasing SRL competence. Consequently, you experience a shift from being a director of learning to acting as a coach. In this role, you discuss learning approaches with students, allowing them to make their own decisions and exercise their learner agency. The payoff is twofold: students become more competent self-regulated learners, and you develop adaptive, responsive teaching practices that cater to these advanced learning needs.

Take action

- Self-evaluate your classroom climate for SRL by reflecting on the characteristics of an SRL classroom in Table 25.
- Enhance your indirect activation of SRL in your classroom by incorporating cooperative learning, constructive learning, autonomous learning or contextualising learning in real life. You may already have aspects of these approaches in your classroom but consider how you might level-up these by incorporating an explicit focus for SRL.

Delve deeper

My website **shyambarr.com/book** includes links to the following resources so you can explore the concepts in this chapter further.

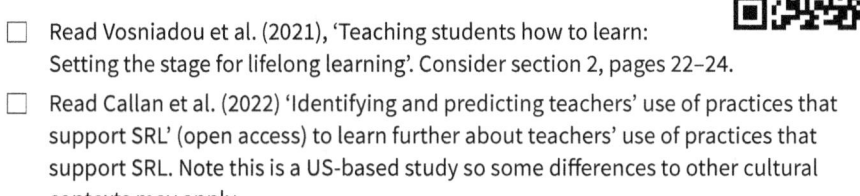

- ☐ Read Vosniadou et al. (2021), 'Teaching students how to learn: Setting the stage for lifelong learning'. Consider section 2, pages 22–24.
- ☐ Read Callan et al. (2022) 'Identifying and predicting teachers' use of practices that support SRL' (open access) to learn further about teachers' use of practices that support SRL. Note this is a US-based study so some differences to other cultural contexts may apply.

Speak like an expert

The 'speak like an expert' strategy is a retrieval practice approach that supports both encoding and retrieval of information from long-term memory. Speaking about a topic from memory helps consolidate knowledge and improves the ability to retrieve information. The strategy reveals the learner's strengths and knowledge gaps, guiding further study, and mimics real-world situations where we must recall and apply knowledge without prompts.

To engage this strategy:

- Without referring to notes, attempt to verbally explain SRL and how to teach it to someone else.
- Focus on articulating what you remember to identify which concepts you can recall easily and which you cannot.
- Use this as a form of retrieval practice to self-evaluate and identify areas for further study.

Applying the strategy in the classroom

- Students can take turns explaining a topic to the class while wearing a 'hat' or another symbol to represent their role as an expert.
- Encourage students to speak confidently and provide feedback on their clarity and content knowledge.

Transfer to other contexts

- Use this strategy to prepare for presentations or public speaking engagements, such as a TEDx Talk, to identify strong points and areas needing improvement.
- Adapt the technique to other subjects or professional development to enhance expertise and confidence in various topics.

PART III
Leading an SRL school improvement initiative

As Alex sees the transformations in her own classroom, she questions how she might have a greater impact beyond the 27 students in front of her. She loves teaching SRL in class, but it seems selfish to keep this wisdom to herself. She wants to see other educators benefit from the knowledge she has gained and, most importantly, to see more students develop the skill set necessary to thrive beyond the school walls. She wants to transform her school into an SRL ecosystem, where SRL is a prominent goal of the school, prioritised within school documents and teacher professional learning and practice.

Adopting a whole-school approach to promoting students' SRL is essential because it ensures consistency and reinforcement of SRL strategies across different subjects and grade levels. A holistic strategy creates a unified educational environment where every stakeholder, from teachers to administrators, is committed to fostering the skills and habits necessary for SRL. It allows for a coordinated effort in embedding SRL practices into the curriculum, extracurricular activities and school culture. Such an approach not only enhances students' learning experiences but also facilitates a deeper and more sustained impact on their ability to self-regulate, adapt and succeed academically and personally.

In this part, I explore the lessons I've learned from my research into whole-school improvement initiatives that emphasise SRL, along with my collaborative experiences with schools. Examining the persistence of these programs and supporting school leaders and educators in their execution has allowed me to witness shared tactics among different schools and the distinct, creative approaches taken by particular establishments. I delve into the complexities of leadership and evaluation necessary to drive a school improvement initiative with a focus on SRL. Beginning with an in-depth analysis of competency-based methods of students' SRL in Chapter 8, I'll then examine effective evaluation instruments, such as surveys, discussion groups and online tracking techniques for students' SRL in Chapter 9. Chapter 10 provides an in-depth look at investigating teachers' knowledge and attitudes, informing an assessment of school readiness and informing future professional learning efforts. Concluding with Chapter 11, this part offers a roadmap for initiating and sustaining a successful SRL program, highlighting strategies that cultivate a robust and flexible educational setting. This part of the book is a comprehensive guide for educational leaders committed to nurturing and measuring SRL within their schools.

8
Assessing SRL: Competency-based learning approaches

What gets measured gets improved.

– Robin Sharma

If the notion 'what gets measured gets improved' rings true, measuring SRL at the year, program or whole-school level is an important step in helping your students self-regulate their learning. This process is crucial not only for formally evaluating the progress of students in SRL, but also for communicating this progress to parents and other stakeholders invested in supporting students' SRL journey. The challenge lies not just in assessing SRL by capturing relevant student data but also in effectively reporting this progress. This chapter delves into the intricacies of SRL assessment and provides insights into how educators can navigate these challenges, ensuring comprehensive and meaningful assessment and reporting of SRL.

Before I share some whole-school approaches to assessing students' SRL, take a moment to reflect on whether and how your school measures and reports on students' SRL by completing Table 28.

Table 28. Evaluation of school assessment of SRL

Is SRL (or aspects of SRL) …	Yes	No	Not sure
… included in some form of behaviour descriptor that teachers report on at the end of the semester?			
… embedded in subject/school rubrics whereby students receive regular feedback on their SRL?			
… incorporated as a student self-assessment, whereby students reflect on their SRL with teachers or as part of parent-teacher-student conferences?			
… integrated with regular student-teacher classroom conversations?			
… considered in a 360-degree approach, whereby students, peers, teachers and perhaps even parents provide feedback regarding a student's SRL progress as a form of high-level calibration?			
… included as a competency-based learning experience whereby students collect evidence of their SRL as part of an e-portfolio?			
… acknowledged in a competency-based learning rubric that teachers use to inform practice but not to formally assess students?			
… assessed using large-scale questionnaires?			
… explored with students through student interviews and focus groups?			
… evaluated using learning analytics (i.e. online trace data)?			

Assessing and reporting on SRL is vital for informing teaching practices, tracking student progress and engaging the educational community. The complexity of SRL, however, means that a diverse range of assessment methods have been explored in research, each with different levels of adoption in schools. In this chapter, I present several practical approaches to assess students' SRL at the year, program and whole-school level, including competency-based learning with a digital portfolio, and a competency rubric with student calibration measures.

Competency-based learning with a digital portfolio

Competency-based learning, in comparison to *content-based learning*, is concerned with students' learning processes. It involves a student 'generating evidence through action or a product that can be used as *evidence of learning*' (Sanford, 2023, p. 190; emphasis added) – in our context, evidence for SRL.

For example, Dickson College (ACT), as part of its 2021–2025 strategic plan, implemented competency-based learning, with a focus on collaboration, communication, creativity, critical thinking and, most recently, confident self-management (remember that self-management is a synonym for SRL). Through an exploration of research literature, school documents and the Australian Curriculum, Margaret O'Donnell, Leader of Student Engagement, and I worked with students to conceptualise what it means to be a 'confident self-manager' (refer Table 29). To better understand the process Margaret and I undertook to define the competency and sub-competencies, follow the link in the delve deeper section of this chapter.

Table 29 shows that *not* all aspects of the SRL knowledge framework (described in Chapter 2) are included. This is due to our explicit focus on behavioural indicators and those aspects that Dickson College students reported they would be able to provide evidence to support. Given the complexity of SRL, it is unreasonable to think that all aspects of SRL can be focused on – this would also create unnecessary cognitive load for students. To make the competency accessible for teachers and students, focus on the aspects of SRL most pertinent to your specific context.

At the time of writing this book in early 2024, the competency and subcompetencies listed in Table 29 had been uploaded to the Mastery Transcript Consortium (https://mastery.org) and are currently being tested with Dickson College students.

Students are able to collect evidence for each sub-competency, get it signed off by college staff (from what I understand, this can be any staff member who can vouch for the student's work) and then submit their evidence to demonstrate each sub-competency, thereby building a portfolio of evidence that demonstrates their capability as a confident self-manager. It's a fantastic process to help students both understand the competency of self-management (and SRL), but to also empower students to take responsibility for their learning.

Table 29. Dickson College's confident self-manager competency and sub-competencies descriptions (as at 6 December 2023), included with permission

Confident self-manager competency description:		
Self-management requires self-awareness and the capability to regulate our behaviours, thoughts and emotions. It happens when we set learning goals, apply learning strategies to achieve those goals, and regularly monitor the effectiveness of our performance. To confidently self-manage, we seek help in order to make progress, complete tasks, overcome obstacles, manage resources and motivate ourselves.		
Sub-competency	**Description**	**Examples of evidence**
Goal-setting and motivation	Through planning, I can effectively analyse a task, set meaningful goals and motivate myself.	• Documented goals • Self-reflection on achieved goals and own weaknesses • Study planner
Time management	I can manage my time including being punctual, prioritising tasks and meeting deadlines.	• A study plan or weekly schedule • Gantt chart • Plan of time organisation • Reflective statement
Help-seeking	I can seek help from others (e.g. peers, teachers, the wider community) or access other appropriate resources to support and improve my progress.	• Participation in study groups (e.g. maths study options) • Drafts submitted with feedback/plan
Learning strategies	I can apply effective learning strategies (e.g. annotating readings, concept mapping, note-taking).	• Notes • Mind maps • Course summary • Annotated reading • Practice questions
Resilience and grit	I can focus my attention and persist when faced with difficult tasks, engaging with learning activities until I make sufficient progress or complete the task.	• Reflective statement
Reflection	I can monitor and evaluate my learning performance and progress against my goals, feedback, assessment criteria and other checkpoints.	• Reflection on assessment feedback or progress against goals
Stress management	I can apply effective strategies to support my wellbeing.	• Reflective statements about productive habits

One concern with this specific competency-based learning approach is that students might begin to view competencies and sub-competencies in a 'tick the box' manner rather than as an ongoing development process. To mitigate this view, consider the developmental progression of the competency itself, ensure that students understand the different criteria for each gradation (discussed in the next section of this chapter) and continuously provide feedback on students' submissions to support a commitment to continuous improvement of the competency. One key benefit of this competency-based learning approach is the explicit teaching of competencies and the requirement for students to identify evidence that is aligned to a specific competency. Therefore, to identify evidence for SRL or SRL strategies, a learner has to understand what SRL is. Examples of students' submissions are included in Figure 20 and Figure 21.

Figure 20. Student example submission – annotated schedule (included with permission)

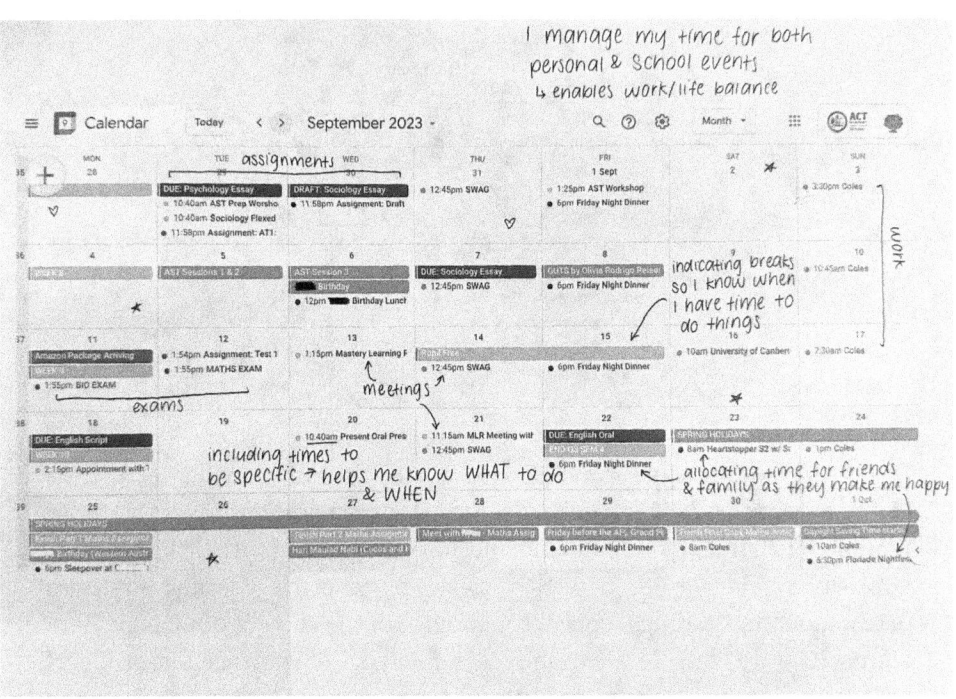

Figure 21. Student example submission – notes from workbook (included with permission)

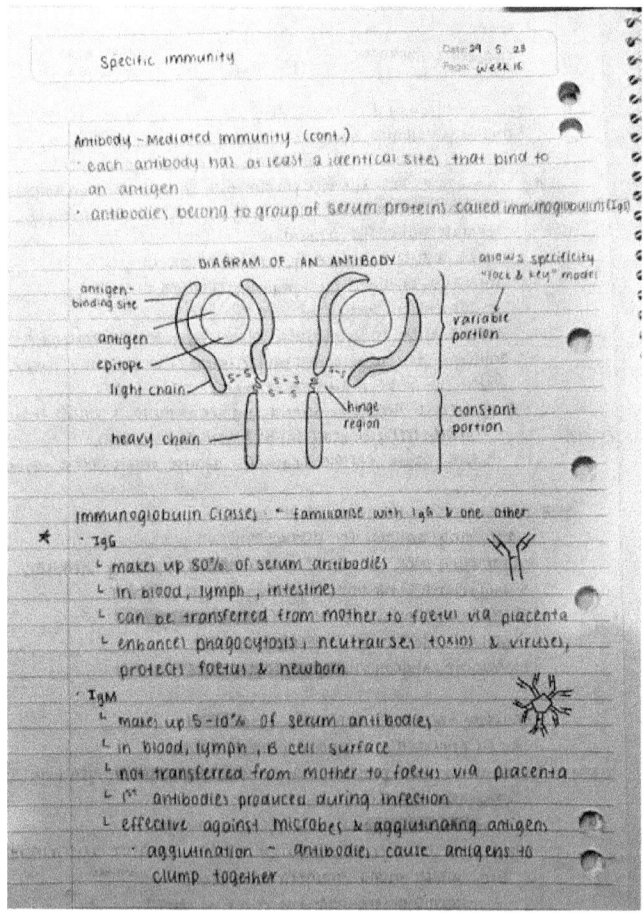

Figure 20 is a student's annotated schedule, providing evidence of their ability to manage their time and demonstrate organisation. Figure 21 is an example of a student's note-taking and how they organise their knowledge. It provides evidence for how they can apply effective learning strategies (e.g. annotating readings, concept mapping) in the subject of biology. Both Figure 20 and Figure 21 are examples of the types of evidence that students have signed off by a college staff member and upload as part of their online portfolio of evidence for the competency of 'confident self-manager'.

As state and territory governments review school certificates (e.g. the South Australian Certificate of Education Learner Profile initiative), and universities begin to move away from traditional measures such as the Australian Tertiary Admission Rank (ATAR) (for example, the University of Melbourne's Australian Learner Competency Credential), having a portfolio of evidence to demonstrate key competencies becomes a learner's résumé of their skills for tertiary studies as well as job applications.

Competency rubric with student calibration measures

You can also take the competency and sub-competencies of SRL and develop a competency rubric – one that assesses specific SRL skills, detailing various levels of proficiency or mastery through clearly defined criteria and performance standards. For at least two decades, it has been argued that rubrics support students' self-assessment (a metacognitive SRL skill) by reducing subjectivity in their assessment and increasing their accuracy (Panadero et al., 2023).

Let's look at an example. Bonython Primary School has a reputation as an inquiry school and has completed substantial work with Kath Murdoch – a leading thinker in implementing inquiry learning. The school uses a learning continuum, which shares similarities with a competency rubric, for the learning asset of self-manager (Murdoch, 2015). Refer Table 30 (overleaf).

From Table 30, you can see that self-manager is broken into eight criteria – all of which cross over with SRL – with gradations occurring across primary school year levels. The rubric supports educators to have conversations with students about their SRL.

Table 30. Learning continuum for the learning asset of self-manager

Throughline	Preschool	Kindergarten	1/2	3/4	5/6
Self as a learner (Personal awareness)	Begin to show awareness of self as a learner	Begin to show awareness of self as a learner by identifying strengths and interests	Show awareness of self as a learner by discussing learning strengths and challenges	Show awareness of self as a learner by identifying and describing strategies that address learning challenges	Act on knowledge of self as a learner by implementing strategies that support learning growth
Perseverance (Perseverance and adaptability)	Have a try before asking for help	Begin to persevere and show grit when experiencing challenges	Persevere and show grit when experiencing challenges	Persevere and show grit when experiencing challenges and with support, adapt approaches based on success	Persevere and show grit when experiencing challenges and adapt approaches based on successes
Goals (Goal-setting)		With support, create goals to assist learning	Set myself simple, short-term goals and reflect on my progress towards them	Plan for learning by setting improvement goals	Select and use strategies to monitor own learning and refine goals to plan for further improvement
Feedback (Reflective practice)		Listen to feedback from educators and peers	Listen to, accept and respond to feedback from educators and peers	Seek, accept and respond to feedback from educators and peers	Seek, respond to and act on feedback from educators and peers

Throughline	Preschool	Kindergarten	1/2	3/4	5/6
Emotions (Emotional awareness and emotional regulation)	Begin to identify emotions and with support, use strategies to regulate emotions	Identify and talk about our emotions with others and with support, use strategies to regulate them	Identify strategies to regulate emotions in familiar contexts	Manage and regulate emotions in familiar contexts using provided strategies	Select and apply appropriate strategies to manage and regulate emotions
Resources	Begin to think about the resources needed for learning	Begin to select and care for personal and shared resources	Select and care for personal and shared resources	Begin to take responsibility for the selection and management of personal and shared resources	Take responsibility for the selection and management of personal and shared resources
Decision-making		Begin to show awareness of how personal choices affect learning	Show awareness of how personal choices affect learning	Make decisions that positively impact on learning	Make decisions and apply strategies that positively impact on learning
Risk-taking and initiative	With support, be open and willing to try new things	Demonstrate willingness to try new things	Identify ways to take risks and challenge self as a learner	With support, take risks and challenge self to improve and grow as a learner	Take risks and challenge self to improve and grow as a learner

DEVELOPED BY BONYTHON PRIMARY SCHOOL WITH KATH MURDOCH (2023), INCLUDED WITH PERMISSION.

Radford College also uses a competency-based learning rubric, building on the International Baccalaureate's (IB's) Approaches to Learning: thinking skills, communication skills, research skills, self-management skills and social skills (IB n.d.). Radford College educators select criteria most relevant to SRL and incorporate this as part of a subject task rubric (refer Figure 22).

Figure 22. Example of Radford College's rubrics for Approaches to Learning, which includes SRL (included with permission)

Year 11 Global Studies

Self-regulation	Demonstrates self-discipline and sets goals	Hudle task interview demonstrates sophisicated inquiry, organisation and application of research, and planning	Hudle task interview demonstrates proficient inquiry, organisation and application of research, and planning	Hudle task interview demonstrates adequate inquiry, organisation and application of research, and planning	Hudle task interview demonstrates developing inquiry, organisation and application of research, and planning	Hudle task interview demonstrates limited inquiry, organisation and application of research, and planning

Year 11 Psychology

Self-regulation	Reflection	Part C – demonstrates a strong sense of self awareness and reflection through the analysis of the strengths and weaknesses of the investigation.	Part C – demonstrates a strong sense of reflection through the analysis of the strengths and weaknesses of the investigation.	Part C – demonstrates a sound sense of reflection through the analysis of the strengths and weaknesses of the investigation.	Part C – demonstrates a developing sense of self awareness and reflection through the analysis of the strengths and weaknesses of the investigation.	Part C – demonstrates a limited sense of self awareness and reflection through the analysis of the strengths and weaknesses of the investigation.

Both teachers and students evaluate student learning using the rubric, which includes an SRL criterion. The evaluation is followed by a 'calibration' conversation, whereby the teacher and student evaluations are placed side by side and a conversation occurs about the similarities and differences. Calibration or judgement accuracy, in the context of SRL, refers to the precision with which students can judge their own learning and performance. This concept involves assessing both relative and absolute accuracy of these judgements. Studies indicate that higher-performing students generally demonstrate greater accuracy in monitoring and evaluating their academic progress. Importantly, training in judgement accuracy within educational courses can lead to more precise self-assessments and improved academic performance (Händel & Dresel, 2022). By continuously having calibration conversations we can support our students in developing their monitoring and judgement accuracy, thus improving their SRL.

Radford College also evaluates SRL during Terms 1 and 3, drawing on students' self-reflections; refer Figure 23.

Figure 23. Examples of Radford College's reporting on students' reflections about their SRL (included with permission)

Year 9 English

Criteria	Strands	Area of strength	Demonstrated	Area for growth
Self-regulation	Demonstrates self-discipline and sets goals	Independently uses time in and out of class to support learning, e.g.: uses note taking strategies effectively; conducts research independently; plans for completion of assigned tasks; and seeks and applies teacher feedback to work.	Uses time in and out of class to support learning, e.g.: takes notes when directed, actively listens and engages in class discussion; and edits and revises work for quality.	Inconsistently uses time in and out of class to support learning, e.g.: partially completes class learning activities; reads portions of texts and relies on summaries.

Year 8 Maths

Criteria	Strands	Area of strength	Demonstrated	Area for growth
Self-regulation	Demonstrates self-discipline and sets goals	Actively engages in class. Helps to create a positive learning environment, independently sets learning goals.	Usually on task and can adjust behaviour independently when required. With guidance, sets realistic learning goals.	Recognises when they should be on task or requires reminding. Requires explicit support to set learning goals.

Figure 23 demonstrates the subject-specific indicators used to evaluate SRL as part of the Radford College Term 1 and Term 3 reporting cycle. While the strand 'demonstrates self-discipline and sets goals' is the same, the descriptors (area of strength, demonstrated and area for growth) vary by subject, acknowledging that self-discipline and goal-setting look different in different subjects. This ensures that students receive valuable feedback that is contextually appropriate. As this is part of a reporting cycle, parents also have access to this information and can support conversations about SRL at home.

Chapter summary

This chapter outlined how implementing competency-based learning approaches can significantly enhance students' SRL. By combining competency-based assessment with portfolios and using competency rubrics with calibration measures, students develop a clearer understanding of learning objectives and can more accurately self-assess their skills and progress. This clarity and self-awareness leads to improved goal-setting, planning and reflection – key components of SRL. Teachers can expect more engaged learners who take ownership of their educational journey, while students gain the ability to self-regulate their learning effectively, resulting in improved academic outcomes.

Take action

- Consider whether your school has a definition for the competency of SRL or similar (e.g. self-management). Is the competency clear for you and students? Are the sub-competencies listed?
- Implement a competency-based learning approach (either combining competency-based assessment with a portfolio or implementing a competency rubric with student calibration measures).

Delve deeper

My website **shyambarr.com/book** includes links to the following resources so you can explore the concepts in this chapter further.

- ☐ Read my blog post to better understand Dickson College's process of defining the competency of self-management.
- ☐ Explore the South Australia Certificate of Education's Learning Profile initiative.
- ☐ Consider the University of Melbourne's Australian Learner Competency Credential.

One word strategy

It's easy to become overwhelmed when presented with so many ideas for how to foster SRL. We can use a one-word strategy to help ground our thinking. Choosing one word focuses attention and serves as a personal mantra for self-regulation and motivation. It fosters a mindful approach to goals and learning. Similar to a pre-commitment strategy, choosing one word is in essence setting an intention.

To implement this strategy:

- Select a single, powerful word that aligns with your core values and encapsulates your intentions and aspirations (or your school's values and aspirations).
- Reflect on why this word is significant to you and how it can guide your behaviour and choices.
- Integrate the word into your daily routine by:
    - Writing it in a visible place where you'll see it regularly.
    - Repeating it to yourself during moments of decision-making or stress.
    - Using it as a touchstone to refocus and recalibrate your actions throughout the day.

Applying the strategy in the classroom

- Guide students to choose their one word to represent their goals or desired personal growth.
- Create activities where students reflect on and share the significance of their chosen word.
- Encourage students to display their word in their learning space as a constant reminder of their focus.

Transfer to other contexts

Use the one word strategy in personal goal-setting, team-building exercises or professional development to maintain alignment with core values.

Embrace the chosen word as a guiding principle during various life transitions or when facing challenges.

Cognitive refresh strategy

At this point in the book, you might be experiencing some high cognitive load as you attempt to make connections to prior knowledge, process new information and consider your goals and strategies for you, your school and your students. Cognitively refreshing your mind, such as stepping away from a task, helps to reduce cognitive load, especially when it's due to processing complex information (germane load). Brief breaks allow the brain to rest and reset, which can enhance decision-making processes and facilitate the formation of meaningful learning schemas.

To implement this strategy:

- Recognise signs of high cognitive load, such as feeling overwhelmed or experiencing mental fatigue.
- Take a deliberate short break from the task at hand, ensuring the break activity is different from the work you've been doing.
- Choose a simple, restful activity for your break, such as:
  - Visiting the restroom.
  - Taking a brief walk, preferably in nature.
  - Practising a few minutes of mindfulness or meditation.

Applying the strategy in the classroom

- Educate students about the signs of high cognitive load and the importance of taking breaks.
- Incorporate short, structured breaks during long learning sessions to improve focus and information retention.
- Provide a quiet space or suggest activities that can serve as a cognitive refresh for students.

Transfer to other contexts

- Apply the step away strategy in various contexts such as during homework sessions, intensive study groups, or even in professional settings where decision-making is critical.
- Encourage the practice of taking short breaks during any mentally demanding task to maintain cognitive performance over time.

9
Assessing SRL: Questionnaires, focus groups and online traces

> Measurement is fabulous. Unless you're busy measuring what's easy to measure as opposed to what's important.
>
> – Seth Godin

As SRL encapsulates many different variables, measuring it is not easy – but it is important. Without an accurate diagnosis of students' current SRL capabilities, our attempts to effectively support students to become self-regulated learners are gambles at best – guestimates rather than evidence-informed decisions. To achieve an evidence-informed decision, we have to gather evidence.

In this chapter, I invite you to:

- leverage an established questionnaire about SRL
- encourage student voice through semi-structured focus groups about SRL
- utilise SRL learning analytics.

Leverage an established questionnaire about SRL

Questionnaires have been used to measure SRL for over three decades, and have been considered 'the most common assessment method in SRL research' (Roth et al., 2016, p. 228). Table 31 documents a selection of SRL questionnaires that you can use to collect data about SRL.

Table 31. Overview of selected SRL questionnaires

Questionnaire	Description	Supporting references
Motivated Strategies for Learning Questionnaire (MSLQ)	The MSLQ was designed to evaluate American college students' motivational beliefs and their use of different learning strategies. The MSLQ is an 81-item measure, taking approximately 20 to 30 minutes. It is divided into 15 scales, which can be used together or separately, depending on the area of investigation. *Question items for the full MSLQ are listed in Pintrich et al., 1991.* Additionally, the MSLQ manual (also publicly available online) includes example feedback sheets for selected scales, a prepared cover and demographics sheets.	Pintrich et al. (1991); Roth et al. (2016).
The junior high school version of the MSLQ	The junior high school version of the MSLQ is a modified version of the full MSLQ. The junior high school version of the MSLQ is a 44-item measure covering motivation, cognitive strategy use, metacognitive strategy use and effort regulation. *Question items for the junior high school version of the MSLQ are listed in Pintrich and De Groot, 1990.*	Chow and Chapman (2017); Pintrich and De Groot (1990); Wang (2012).

Questionnaire	Description	Supporting references
Metacognitive Awareness Inventory (MAI) or Junior Metacognitive Awareness Inventory	The MAI was designed to investigate students' metacognition, including a focus on the planning, monitoring, and evaluating phases of SRL, and different strategy categories. The MAI is a 52-item measure, originally used with college students. The Junior MAI was designed to evaluate metacognition in children in Grades 3-9 (Version A, 12 items for Grades 3-5; Version B, 18 items for Grades 6-9). *Question items for the original MAI are listed in Schraw & Dennison (1994).*	Schraw and Dennison (1994).
Motivation and Engagement Scale (MES)	*Note: this questionnaire is a paid service.* The MES is a 44-item survey assessing each part of the Motivation and Engagement Wheel (https://lifelongachievement.com/pages/the-wheel). There are 11 parts to the wheel, categorised under positive motivation, positive engagement, negative motivation and negative engagement. There are three parallel versions: MES – Junior School (elementary/primary), MES – High School, and MES – University/College. Each version has demonstrated reliability and validity. The MES takes 10 to 15 minutes to complete (in class, in groups, or individually). It is available as an online form or a PDF form, and further information can be found at: https://lifelongachievement.com/pages/the-motivation-and-engagement-scale-mes	Liem and Martin (2012); Martin (2009); Martin (2007); Martin (2023).

As you can see from Table 31, there are multiple established questionnaires in the field of SRL. So, where do you start? Consider the following:

- What do you want to achieve with a questionnaire?
  - Is there a particular aspect of students' SRL that you wish to explore?
  - Do you want to get a broad sense for how students self-regulate their learning?
- How much time do you (and others) have available for this?
- What's your timeline?
- What's your budget (if any)?

The other thing to consider prior to implementing a questionnaire is that you may already be using a questionnaire that has indicators for students' SRL that you could draw on as a starting point (without implementing a new survey altogether). For example, when leaders from Radford College first approached me to support the school's aspirations for SRL, they were drawing on data from the Tell Them From Me survey (a survey that measures student engagement and wellbeing) currently used in NSW. The data raised concerns about students' motivation and engagement, so our initial entry point was to look into how we could help students to better self-regulate their own motivation for learning.

If the data already available is insufficient to inform next steps for students' SRL, then you can implement an 'off-the-shelf' questionnaire or a 'done-for-you' questionnaire.

An 'off-the-shelf' questionnaire

Depending on the nature of your inquiry into SRL, you might look to implement a validated and established questionnaire (e.g. the junior high school version of the MSLQ). When implementing an 'off-the-shelf' questionnaire, consider the following:

- Who will complete the questionnaire? (Year level? Age group?)
- When will they complete it? (In class? During a specific lesson?)
- Will it occur in specific subjects or varied subjects?
- How will you analyse the data?

A 'done-for-you' questionnaire service

The MES by the Lifelong Achievement Group is an example of a 'done-for-you' service. You request the service, indicate which survey you'd like to use (primary, secondary or tertiary), how many students will participate and when the surveys will be conducted, and the Lifelong Achievement Group will provide you with the necessary survey links and the instructions for students at the time of sitting. The Lifelong Achievement Group also processes and analyses the data, minimising the amount of work you must complete. The MES also includes feedback to students along with worksheets and instructions for how to improve different aspects of their SRL. For sample MES survey items/pages, data spreadsheets and student profile sheets, visit https://lifelongachievement.com/pages/the-motivation-and-engagement-scale-mes.

Conduct a student focus group around SRL

If you're concerned about survey fatigue, you might choose to conduct a focus group to gather insights into learners' SRL experiences. Focus groups enable participants to provide responses that go beyond the questions specifically mentioned in a questionnaire, and allow the facilitator to probe participants' responses for further information (e.g. 'Tell me more about that', 'What makes you say that?') (Creswell & Guetterman, 2019).

Focus groups can be used to gather information about students' conceptual and strategic knowledge about SRL and their SRL behaviours. For example:

- Students' conceptual and strategic knowledge about SRL:
  - 'Describe SRL.'
  - 'What types of things do you need to know to engage in SRL?'
- Students' SRL behaviours:
  - 'What do you do when X happens?'
  - 'What does it look like when someone is engaged in SRL?'
- Students' motivation and strategies to self-motivate:
  - 'How do you know when you are lacking motivation?'
  - 'What do you do to motivate yourself for learning?'

You can also use focus groups to gather insights about students' perceptions of teaching practice about SRL. Radford College explored this during 2023, conducting three focus groups, each with around six students from mixed-year-level groups. The focus groups were designed to generate information for the following three questions/prompts:

1. Describe your experience of learning SRL in the classroom.
2. How has this affected your learning? How beneficial has it been?
3. What might your teachers do to help you better self-regulate your learning?

The focus group session plan is outlined in Table 32.

Table 32. Focus group session plan at Radford College

Activity	Time
Welcome – Leader/Teacher to contextualise session; Shyam introduction.	5
Provide students with post-it notes. On the **top half** of post-it notes, individually, students generate responses to the following questions: Imagine that I was sitting in your classroom. Tell me: 1. What might I hear your teacher saying? 2. What might I see your teacher doing? Note: Each teacher statement or action is written on a separate post-it note.	10
In your own words, what does it mean to be a self-regulated learner? Discuss as a group and generate a shared definition.	10
On the **bottom half** of the post-it note: Rate each teacher statement or action on a scale of 1–10 (1. Doesn't support me as a self-regulated learner; 10. Supports my capability as a self-regulated learner) and explain your reasoning for the chosen score. If time allows, discuss and sort.	10
In addition to what has already been mentioned, what might your teachers say and/or do to better help you develop as a self-regulated learner? Discuss as a group.	10
Questions and gratitude for participation/contribution.	5

Starting at the top of Table 32, moving beyond the 'welcome', there is a series of generation-type activities used to help activate students' prior knowledge about SRL and ensure a shared understanding. The lower half of Table 32 focuses on students generating and prioritising different teaching actions based on their perceived effectiveness for supporting students' SRL.

When conducting focus groups, be mindful of the following:

- **Learners' verbal competencies:** Focus groups typically require verbal responses to questions, so age and development is a consideration. This approach might not be suitable for younger learners, although getting these students to express their understanding through drawing or

creative exercises might offer an interesting insight into their developing conception of what it means to be learner.
- **Demand characteristics:** Students may feel the need to state what they think the teacher/facilitator wants to hear, rather than their honest responses. To mitigate this, create a culture of psychological safety by emphasising the importance of respecting learners' responses and your interest in hearing genuine and honest insights from students.

Utilise online analytics

While questionnaires and focus groups are great for gathering data on students' SRL, they are dependent on student perceptions which bring with them a level of subjective variability and make it difficult to measure SRL as a process. An alternative, and arguably more authentic, approach is to use online analytics. Most schools have an online platform where course and unit learning materials are stored (e.g. Google Classroom, Canvas, Compass, Schoolbox). These online platforms generate analytic data about students' engagement in learning that occurs online.

By considering students' behaviours/interactions with digital learning environments, you can gain insights into your students' learning behaviours, such as time management, resource usage and engagement patterns. This data can reveal how students approach learning tasks, allowing you to tailor interventions and support individual learning needs more effectively. Additionally, it provides a basis for discussions with students about their learning strategies, fostering a deeper understanding and improvement of their SRL skills. Here are some questions to ask about online analytics:

- Do you have access to online analytics about students' learning?
- Do you use the online analytics to inform judgements of students' SRL?
- How might you use online analytics to build a more holistic picture of students' SRL?

Consider the online analytics available to you and whether this data aligns with SRL concepts, strategies and behaviours. For an example of different online analytics and how they align to SRL, refer Table 33.

Table 33. Example of online SRL behavioural indicators

SRL phase	Examples of online analytics
Planning	• Setting or modifying goals; planning learning strategies and time to reach goals. • Completing learning tasks at least one to three days earlier than due dates; skipping (<15 s), skimming through (15–35 s) or engaging in (>35 s) the tasks during initial attempt. • Viewing course information page, syllabus with course details, resources, task lists or summaries.
Monitoring	• Starting, viewing, or submitting quizzes, assignments or forums; showing the answers or outcome of quizzes or assignments. • Accessing learning material pages (e.g. video lecture) then passing or attempting quizzes or discussions. • Outlining or managing hypotheses; adding tests; searching library.
Evaluating	• Evaluating the performance of time planning, performing strategy or completing goals. • Number of visits to events or course resources, quizzes, submitted assignments or updated submissions. • Interactions with course details page or progress page after taking quizzes.

ADAPTED FROM DU ET AL. (2023, P. 7).

By analysing the online analytics associated with the planning phase, you can identify students who are proactive in setting and modifying their learning goals, as well as those who may need guidance on time management and strategy planning. For instance, students completing tasks ahead of deadlines suggests effective SRL planning behaviours, while those skimming through tasks might need support in developing more in-depth engagement strategies.

During the monitoring phase, you can observe student engagement through their interactions with quizzes, assignments and learning materials. Those who frequently start or view assignments but do not submit them may be facing challenges that require additional support or intervention. The analytics can also show if the learning materials are effectively aiding students in their preparation for assessments, allowing you to adjust the resources accordingly.

Finally, in the evaluating phase, analytics can inform you about students' self-assessment skills. Regular visits to course resources and interactions with progress pages post-quizzes indicate a student's inclination to reflect on their performance. This information can be used to praise self-evaluative behaviours or to introduce self-assessment strategies to those who might not engage in such practices.

Overall, these analytics serve as a feedback mechanism for you to tailor your instruction and provide targeted support to foster students' self-regulatory skills in an online learning environment.

Chapter summary

In this chapter we investigated three key approaches for assessing SRL: leveraging established questionnaires, conducting semi-structured focus groups and utilising SRL learning analytics. These methods offer you a comprehensive view of your students' SRL abilities, enabling the adoption of targeted instructional strategies. For students, these assessments provide valuable feedback on their learning processes, promoting self-awareness and growth in SRL competencies. This chapter highlighted the benefits of integrating these assessment approaches into teaching practices, enhancing both teaching efficacy and student learning outcomes.

Take action

Each approach listed in Chapters 8 and 9 has pros and cons. I presented them as options; however, I recommend combining multiple modes of assessment so that you can build an informed picture of students' SRL.

- Consider what assessment and reporting approaches for SRL already exist in your school:
    - What data do you have that informs a picture of students' SRL?
    - What data is missing from your picture of students' SRL?
- Choose one (or more) assessment and feedback approach(es) that best suits your school context and the aim of the inquiry into students' SRL:
    - Combine competency-based assessment with a portfolio.
    - Implement a competency rubric with student calibration measures.
    - Use a large-scale questionnaire.
    - Expand with student interviews and focus groups.
    - Incorporate online analytics data.

- If possible, use multiple modes of assessment to try to capture a more holistic picture of students' SRL *or* focus on a small part of the SRL picture (e.g. motivation) and use an assessment method that might give you accurate information about that particular component.

Delve deeper

My website **shyambarr.com/book** includes links to the following resources so you can explore the concepts in this chapter further.

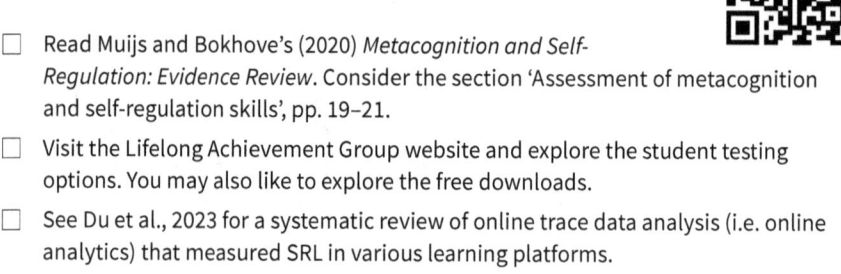

- ☐ Read Muijs and Bokhove's (2020) *Metacognition and Self-Regulation: Evidence Review*. Consider the section 'Assessment of metacognition and self-regulation skills', pp. 19–21.
- ☐ Visit the Lifelong Achievement Group website and explore the student testing options. You may also like to explore the free downloads.
- ☐ See Du et al., 2023 for a systematic review of online trace data analysis (i.e. online analytics) that measured SRL in various learning platforms.

SRL TOOLBOX

Win list strategy

At this point, you may have implemented some changes in your school, so it's a good time to celebrate the small wins using a win list strategy. A 'win list' is a compilation of achievements, successes or positive outcomes, often used in personal or professional contexts. It serves as a motivational strategy and a record of accomplishments. Creating a win list reinforces self-efficacy by acknowledging past successes and the strategies that led to them. Furthermore, it helps to build a positive mindset by counteracting negativity bias and sets a precedent for achieving future goals.

To create a win list:

- Start by reflecting on all your teaching experiences related to SRL or the successes you have had with gathering information about students' SRL
- Write down every success related to SRL, no matter the size; include student progress, teaching methods you've implemented, and productive discussions about SRL.
- Continually ask yourself, 'What else can I list?' to extend the list.

Applying the strategy in the classroom

- Encourage students with low self-efficacy to create their own win lists for your subject.
- Facilitate discussions on past successes and the feelings, strategies and resources that contributed to those achievements.
- Help students connect those past winning strategies to their current tasks and challenges.

Transfer to other contexts

- Apply the win list approach to other subjects, professional development or personal goals to consistently build and maintain a sense of accomplishment.
- Use win lists in team settings to foster a culture of recognition and shared success.
- Regularly update and review win lists to motivate perseverant effort through new challenges and to promote lifelong resilience.

10
Exploring teachers' SRL knowledge, beliefs and practice

Beliefs influence what teachers say and do in class.
— Frank Pajares

Recognising the importance of SRL in student education, it is imperative for leaders to also focus on the educators – the architects of learning. Effective leadership involves viewing teachers not just as facilitators but as learners themselves. This perspective necessitates a preliminary, diagnostic assessment of educators' current understanding and application of SRL principles. Such an evaluation serves as a cornerstone for tailored professional development. We will explore a variety of methodologies, including questionnaires, focus groups and classroom observations, to gather comprehensive insights into teachers' perspectives on SRL. The aim is to support teachers by creating bespoke professional learning programs. These programs are not only beneficial for the teachers' professional growth, but are instrumental in fostering an environment where both students and educators engage in a continuous, reflective learning process. By doing so, leaders and teachers collectively model a dynamic learning journey, emphasising the importance of feedback, adaptation and progressive improvement in educational practices.

There are multiple ways to gather information about teachers' SRL knowledge, beliefs and practice. In this chapter, I invite you to:

- conduct a teacher questionnaire about SRL
- consult teachers via informal conversations, one-on-one meetings and focus groups
- explore SRL teaching practice using lesson observations.

Conduct a teacher questionnaire about SRL

As mentioned in Chapter 9, questionnaires or surveys are common practice in schools as they are convenient to conduct with large groups and can be efficient in terms of processing and analysis. There are several questionnaires that explore teachers' thinking and practice about SRL; refer Table 34.

Table 34. Selected questionnaires about teachers' SRL knowledge, beliefs and practice

Questionnaire	Description	Supporting references
Self-Regulated Learning Teacher Belief Scale (SRLTB)	The SRLTB is a 10-item self-report scale that assesses teachers' beliefs about the teaching SRL in primary schools. Teachers respond on a five-point Likert scale. *Question items for the SRLTB are listed in Lombaerts et al. (2009).*	Lombaerts et al. (2009).
Teacher Self-Efficacy Scale to implement SRL (TSES-SRL)	The TSES-SRL investigates teachers' self-efficacy and teaching practice about SRL. The TSES-SRL requires educators to respond to 24 question items on a five-point Likert scale. *Question items for the TSES are listed in De Smul et al. (2018).*	De Smul et al. (2018).

Questionnaire	Description	Supporting references
Beliefs About Learning and Teaching (BALT)	The BALT explores teachers' beliefs about learning and teaching that are both consistent and inconsistent with SRL. It includes 73 items around teachers' beliefs that influence teaching practice about SRL. *Question items for the full BALT are listed in Vosniadou et al. (2020). Please note a shortened version of the BALT was used by Darmawan et al. (2020), and more recently in Fischer and Dignath (2023).*	Vosniadou et al. (2020).
Teachers' Epistemic Cognition about SRL (TEC-SRL)	The TEC-SRL was designed to gather information about factors (e.g. knowledge, beliefs) that influence teachers' decision-making processes related to promoting SRL in lessons. The TEC-SRL includes Likert-scale items and open-ended questions, and takes around 30 minutes to complete. *Question items for the full TEC-SRL are listed in Barr (2021). Please contact me via www.shyambarr.com if you are interested in the TEC-SRL question items.*	Barr (2021).

Table 34 offers a selection of questionnaires that have been used to investigate teachers' knowledge, beliefs and practices about SRL.

Given the complexity of some of these questionnaires, I see three options to move forward. Firstly, you can implement a validated and established questionnaire. For example, you might use the SRLTB (Lombaerts et al., 2009), noting that the questionnaires have been validated more recently in different educational settings (e.g. Dignath-van Ewijk & van der Werf, 2012). Teachers scoring high on the SRLTB are considered promoters of SRL. An alternative option is to curate a selection of questions of interest from a range of established questionnaires. Lastly, if budget allows, you might engage a researcher to support you in the selection and execution of a teacher questionnaire about SRL, including data analysis and summary reports of findings. However, such an exercise can be an expensive option. No matter the approach, here are some considerations:

- How much time do you (and others) have available for administering and completing questionnaires?

- What's your timeline? When do you require the information, and when will the administering and analysis of the questionnaire occur?
- What's your budget (if any)?
- Who will complete the questionnaire? Some or all teachers?
- When will teachers complete it?

Consult with teachers

Speaking to teachers is an effective method to gain insights about teachers' SRL thinking and practice. You can gain these insights through relatively informal conversations with staff whether that be in the day-to-day functioning of the school, or through one-on-one meetings. For example, in one of my earliest research studies (Barr & Askell-Williams, 2020), I explored the changes in the quality of four secondary school science teachers' SRL knowledge, beliefs and practice as they participated in an SRL professional learning program. Pre- and post- the professional learning program, I used semi-structured interviews to capture different elements of teachers' SRL knowledge, beliefs and practice. The interview questions I used are listed in Table 35.

Table 35. Semi-structured interview protocol

Question 1. • How would you describe SRL? • How would you describe the SRL behaviour of your students at this moment? • On a scale of 1–10 (10 being a self-regulated learner), how would you rate the majority of students in your class? Why?
Question 2. • What are the best ways to enhance students' SRL behaviours? • Which of these have you been able to implement in your classroom? • What have been the challenges?
Question 3. • In your lessons do you explicitly teach your students about SRL? • If answer is 'NO', what makes you say that? • If answer is 'YES', what is it that you do? Why do you do that? How often do you do that?

> **Question 4.**
> - In your teaching you teach students about subject matter – a complex body of detailed knowledge about a curriculum area such as science. Is there a similarly complex body of knowledge about SRL?
>   – If 'YES': What are some of the key areas of knowledge about SRL? Where do we find that knowledge?
>   – If 'NO': Why do you think there isn't such a complex body of knowledge about SRL?
> - Do you have a similar depth of knowledge in these two areas – of science and SRL? Why or why not?
> - Do your students have a similar depth of knowledge in these two areas – of science and SRL? Why or why not?
> - Do you think students need the same *depth* of knowledge about these two areas to learn effectively in your lessons?
>
> **Question 5.**
> - When I have talked with teachers about SRL strategies, some of them say that spending time in class lessons teaching SRL strategies is not as useful for the students as spending the time teaching them about subject matter content. What is your view on this? Do you agree with the view put forward by that group of teachers? Explain why you agree or disagree.

ADAPTED FROM BARR & ASKELL-WILLIAMS (2020).

Conversations with teachers about SRL demand a careful combination of techniques for eliciting in-depth and accurate responses:

- **Probing:** Invite teachers to expand on their responses using prompts such as 'tell me more about that' or 'what makes you say that?'.
- **Paraphrasing:** Invite teachers to review and clarify their responses so you can check for accuracy of understanding.

Given the difficulties in conducting individual one-on-one meetings in schools (logistics with timetables, pulling teachers from classes), focus groups that leverage a similar set of questions offer a more efficient approach to gathering insights about teachers' SRL thinking and practice. One novel focus group approach I witnessed at the University of Canberra (ACT) was 'coffee mornings'. Researchers invited staff to join them for a free coffee at a local cafe at certain times throughout the day, to share their thoughts about certain initiatives at the university. This approach could be leveraged in schools to explore what teachers think about SRL. Alternatively, you could conduct a focus group about SRL during a team meeting or a professional learning session with leaders facilitating and collecting the information for different table groups.

Evaluate SRL teaching behaviours using the ATES instrument

Lesson observations provide an accurate assessment of SRL teaching behaviour (e.g. explicit strategy instruction, metacognitive prompting, providing opportunities to practise SRL).

The Assessing How Teachers Enhance Self-Regulated Learning (ATES) observation instrument (Dignath et al., 2022) is used to assess SRL teaching practice including the classroom environment for SRL, and has been proven valid and reliable in German, Swiss, Flemish and Australian schools. The ATES instrument is used to code video-recorded lessons – efficiently achieved in schools by using video-capturing technology (e.g. iPads, Swivl). Once recorded, a coder watches the video and allocates each 1-minute segment to different categories (e.g. stimulating metacognitive reflection, activation of transfer, explicit instruction, implicit instruction, metacognitive strategies, cognitive strategies, motivation for strategy use) (Dignath-van Ewijk, Dickhäuser, & Büttner, 2013; Dignath et al., 2022). Refer Table 36 for an example of the spreadsheet.

From Table 36, you can see that each minute of the lesson is listed on the left-hand side, while examples of the ATES categories are listed at the top. Once you have coded the different teaching behaviours, you can calculate the time spent on each category and compare it to a teacher's previous performance (personal progress), a mean of other teachers at the school (social comparison), or to samples of educators from previous research studies that have used the ATES instrument (e.g. Barr, 2021; Dignath et al., 2022).

Table 36. Sample spreadsheet of ATES instrument

Time	Explicit teacher instruction	Implicit teacher instruction	Type of strategy (MC, C, M or general)	Specified type of strategy	Clarifying benefit of strategy use	Activating transfer of strategy use	Teaching metacognition/ SRL or stimulating metaccognitive reflection	Comments
0:00–1:00								
1:00–2:00								
2:00–3:00								
3:00–4:00								

4:00–5:00									
5:00–6:00									
6:00–7:00									
7:00–8:00									
8:00–9:00									
9:00–10:00									
10:00–11:00									
11:00–12:00									

FROM DIGNATH-VAN EWIJK, DICKHÄUSER, & BÜTTNER (2013) AND DIGNATH ET AL. (2022), INCLUDED WITH PERMISSION.

Given the requirement to video-record lessons and code minute-by-minute, using the ATES instrument can be a time-consuming activity. I suggest modifying the ATES for the more typical classroom observation and feedback cycles that occur in schools. For example, rather than video-record a lesson, an observer might enter a classroom with the specific focus of collecting data in the lesson related to the explicit instruction of SRL strategies. The observer might take notes about the different strategy instruction that occurs and then reflect on the observations using the titles in the columns of the ATES instrument (refer Table 36). Feedback would then incorporate reference to the ATES observation instrument, including the different approach to explicit teaching strategies (e.g. explanation, demonstration, inquiry, call).

Chapter summary

This chapter explored the ways in which leaders can deepen their understanding of teachers' SRL knowledge, beliefs and practices. It presented various methods, including questionnaires, focus groups and classroom observations centred on SRL. These strategies allow leaders to gain a deeper understanding of teachers' perspectives on SRL, which in turn, helps them to tailor professional development programs to meet their educators' specific needs. Such programs are designed with the direct intent to benefit teachers as learners. For students, the benefit lies in leaders and teachers modelling a process of learning, including receiving and acting on feedback and planning improvement for practice.

Take action

- Choose a data-gathering process to help diagnose teachers' challenges with teaching SRL and inform professional learning experiences. Keep in mind time and budget, as some data-gathering tools require either financial or human resources.
- Investigate the questionnaires available and construct a suitable questionnaire to investigate teachers' thinking at your school.
- Consider running an interview or focus group to explore teachers' thinking about SRL.
- Explore how you can incorporate aspects of the ATES instrument in the lesson observations and feedback cycles at your school.

Delve deeper

My website **shyambarr.com/book** includes links to the following resources so you can explore the concepts in this chapter further.

- ☐ Revisit Lawson et al.'s (2018) paper 'Teachers' and Students' Belief Systems About the Self-Regulation of Learning'.
- ☐ Watch my 'Beliefs that get in the way of teaching SRL' video.
- ☐ Revisit the 'Assessing How Teachers Enhance Self-Regulated Learning Coding Guide' (Dignath et al., 2022) and consider its use for evaluating lesson observations and teacher behaviours.

The mastery focus strategy

Having a mastery rather than a performance orientation is important, because mastery focuses on the process and the development of competence. This has been demonstrated in multiple educational settings (Bruning et al., 2010). According to Fishbach and Choi's (2012) study, adopting a mastery focus can lead to more substantial and sustainable achievements. For example, individuals concentrating on the process of mastering an exercise technique were more successful in losing weight than those who merely focused on the outcome of weight loss. This suggests that a mastery orientation, which values learning and skill acquisition, can inadvertently lead to achieving performance goals, because it encourages a deeper engagement with the task and persistence in the face of challenges.

To implement the mastery focus strategy in relation to SRL, set the following goals for teaching and/or leading SRL (maybe it's your own goal for teaching or leading SRL, or it's a goal regarding teachers' SRL practice):

- Performance goal (i.e. the end goal, a performance measurement)
  - E.g. number of minutes spent explicitly teaching SRL strategies, set target in a performance appraisal.
- Mastery goal (i.e. the steps required to bring about your desired performance)
  - E.g. setting a learning intention for SRL each lesson; practising the explicit teaching of SRL strategies before a task; dedicating 10 minutes a day to engage in professional learning about teaching SRL, such as reading this book.

Applying the strategy in the classroom

Encourage students to set performance and mastery goals. Performance goals for students might include achieving high grades, while mastery goals are about the learning process, such as developing certain skills or understanding concepts deeply. Encourage students to use journals for reflection on these goals and promote collaborative dialogue to differentiate and balance performance and mastery objectives. Once set, encourage students to focus on the mastery goal.

Transfer to other contexts

If your students or you have set goals beyond the classroom, how might focusing on the mastery of skills, rather than just the achievement of an endpoint, enhance the journey and lead to a deeper understanding or more profound success? Reflect on how prioritising the learning process can be beneficial in various settings, such as in sports, arts or personal development.

11
Launching a whole-school SRL initiative

The whole is greater than the sum of its parts.

— Gestalt theory

Integrating individual insights into a cohesive strategy amplifies their impact. With the robust data you've collected on your students' SRL, coupled with your diagnostic assessment of teachers' perspectives on SRL, you are in a prime position to orchestrate a school-wide initiative that focuses on enhancing SRL.

In this chapter, I invite you to:

- communicate a strong focus on SRL
- craft a rich professional learning experience about SRL
- seek and share feedback about the SRL initiative
- acknowledge schools as complex adaptive systems.

Communicate a strong focus on SRL

Communicating your focus on SRL is essentially clarifying *why* educators at your school should care about SRL and the teaching of SRL.

To effectively communicate your *why* for SRL, include the following in your message:

- evidence of the benefits of SRL (refer Chapter 1; e.g. SRL is associated with high achievement and is an essential skill for the future of work)

- evidence from student data about SRL (e.g. 'recent surveys we've conducted at the school have demonstrated that there is an opportunity for students in Year X to better self-regulate their learning')
- a clear positioning of SRL within the school context, such as connections to the school's vision, mission, values, strategic intent and so on.

For example, Louise Wallace-Richards, Assistant Principal Teaching and Learning at Radford College, justified a focus on SRL using student data from the Tell Them From Me survey (NSW), the IB's Approaches to Learning, and the school's learner traits which include an explicit focus on being self-regulated. Refer Figure 24.

Figure 24. Radford College learner traits (included with permission)

On the left of Figure 24 we see an overview of the Radford learner traits, with the learner trait of self-regulated expanded on the right.

Other schools have leveraged different surveys, used school documents such as a strategic plan or connected a focus on SRL to the school's values. Refer Table 37 for some examples.

Table 37. Examples of other SRL school initiatives aligned to school documents, policies and goals

School	Initiative	Alignment to school documents
Melbourne Girls Grammar (Vic) 2015–2017	• Professional learning about SRL with middle-leadership • Development of a transition program for the (at the time) new Senior Years 9–12 program	• School value: self-discipline • School strategic intent: focus on personalised learning and student agency • School survey data: Motivation and Engagement Scale • School professional learning focus: partnership with Flinders University
Dickson College (ACT) 2021–current	• Self-management project	• School improvement plan 2021–2025: Priority 2: improve students' self-management capability
Bonython Primary School (ACT) 2021–current	• Developing a goal-setting culture; enabling students to do the 'heavy lifting'	• School learner asset: Self-Manager; Thinker • School improvement plan 2022-2026: Improve students' goal-setting

Based on the examples provided in Table 37, what connections and alignment exist at your school to strongly position a focus on SRL?

Craft a rich professional learning experience about SRL

A critical component of an SRL school improvement initiative is the development of staff expertise. To achieve this necessitates a shift from traditional, isolated professional development approaches – often likened to brief, one-day 'espresso shots' of inspiration with minimal long-term impact – to more comprehensive professional education that meets a number of quality indicators. Refer Table 38. The five quality indicators in Table 38 continue to be used by researchers investigating the effectiveness of professional education interventions (e.g. Barr, 2021; Heirweg et al., 2022), hence they have been selected for this book.

Building on these quality indicators, whole-school approaches to promoting SRL incorporate different levels of learning (different groups of learners), feature different professional learning experiences and are designed for longevity. Let's look at each of these factors.

Table 38. Quality indicators of effective professional education

Quality indicator	Description
Content focus	Focus learning in specific subject matter and how students learn this content (e.g. SRL processes, including motivational, cognitive and metacognitive strategies).
Active learning	Involve teachers in discussions, lesson observations and feedback cycles. Ensure teachers are actively constructing knowledge rather than being passive recipients of information.
Coherence	Align professional education with school documents (policies, vision etc.) and teachers' goals (e.g. attainment goals, curriculum guidelines).
Duration	Spread professional education over a longer period of time, with '20 or more hours of contact time spread over an entire semester considered the benchmark' (Heirweg et al., 2022, p. 931).
Collective participation	Involve leaders and teachers from different levels to enable contextualised discussions and increased cooperation between teams.

ADAPTED FROM DESIMONE, 2009.

Incorporate different levels of learning

Firstly, whole-school approaches to SRL should include professional education embedded at multiple levels within the school; refer Table 39.

Finding ways to meaningfully engage the different levels is important in the sustainability of school improvement initiatives (Koh et al., 2023), but primarily because it ensures a unified approach to education, where everyone is aligned with the school's goals and teaching methods.

Table 39. Whole-school approaches to engage different stakeholders in learning about SRL

Level	Melbourne Girls Grammar (2016–2017)	Radford College (2019–2024)	Bonython Primary School (2021–2024)
Leadership	Presentations to leadership – continuous update of project progress.	Year-long focus with senior and middleleaders.	Leadership focus group (continuous).

Level	Melbourne Girls Grammar (2016–2017)	Radford College (2019–2024)	Bonython Primary School (2021–2024)
Teachers	Staff involved in professional learning partnership with Flinders University.	Whole staff professional learning, communities of practice, faculty visits.	Teachers as Researchers group, all-staff workshops, teacher focus group, educator inquiries.
Students	Teachers translate into practice, student transition program to Senior Years program.	Teachers translate into practice, Shyam presented on attention regulation, student focus groups.	Teachers translate into practice, Shyam visited classrooms, Empowered Leaders Conference.
Parents	Parent education series (presentations to parents about SRL).	School newsletter, academic forums with parent reps.	Communication with the community is framed using the language of SRL and the learning assets through different channels (e.g. social media, Seesaw and school reports).

Feature different professional learning experiences

Effective professional education in schools also features various professional learning experiences, such as direct and explicit instruction, active learning (i.e. opportunities to practise new strategies), collective participation, and 'the prerequisite tools to successfully implement the intervention' (Bouwer et al., 2017, p. 3). Examples of the diversity of professional learning experiences is evident in Table 39. In addition to those listed, and drawing on a collaboration with the Association of Independent Schools ACT (AISACT), I also suggest the following options:

- **Framing Directions full-day:** A full-day experience at the beginning of the initiative that 'frames up' the year by activating prior knowledge, generating guiding questions and establishing the direction of the experience based on the group.
- **Online learning modules:** Videos, readings and online activities that participants work through independently or in their school teams.
- **Group coaching sessions:** Teams of teachers come together and share challenges with the content and gain clarity through discussion. In the

AISACT collaboration, I facilitate the group coaching sessions; however, a suitable coach within the school environment could also facilitate such conversations (e.g. leaders, instructional coach).
- **In-school meetings:** As the AISACT collaboration involves multiple schools, this allows me to work directly with school teams to help problem-solve implementation in context (e.g. evaluate progress, set goals and select processes to move forward). This would be suitable for large schools with multiple campuses, or schools with different programs (e.g. junior school, middle school and/or senior school).

Dedicate time and design for longevity

When planning SRL professional education in schools, it's important to think about how much time you'll need. Enough time must be allowed not just for learning about SRL, but also for putting it into practice and checking to see how well it works. This means making sure your schedule gives teachers and staff plenty of opportunities to fully understand and apply SRL concepts in the classroom. Time must be allocated to:

- learning about the new initiative
- planning its application
- integrating it into the curriculum
- reviewing its effectiveness.

Researchers have advocated that the success of professional education hinges on the 'dosage' of education – the number of hours or sessions and the overall timeframe of the program. For example, Yoon et al. (2007) found that primary school teachers who underwent more than 14 hours of professional development achieved notable student performance improvements. Similarly, Piasta et al. (2010) observed enhanced literacy teaching practices among preschool teachers following an 11-hour professional development intervention. Recently, Heirweg et al. (2022) stated that professional development programs 'of 20 or more hours of contact time spread over an entire semester are considered the benchmark' (p. 931).

From practical experience, I've found the most effective professional learning experiences meet this 'dosage' requirement, but also span at least three years, offering varying engagement levels throughout. This duration allows for a deeper understanding, thoughtful implementation and thorough evaluation, leading to better educational outcomes. For example, Radford College started its implementation of an SRL school improvement initiative in 2019; it has dedicated time and designed a school improvement initiative for longevity. Refer Table 40.

Table 40. Overview of Radford College's approach to SRL professional learning

2019 Identifying the opportunity	2020 Establishing interest/value	2021 Learning and sharing	2022-2023 Learning and sharing	2024 Learning and sharing
• School document: Learner trait of self-regulated. • Tell Them From Me survey data (student data): motivation and engagement.	• Introductory sessions with whole school (ELC–12) and leaders. • Academic forum (board, parents etc.).	• Professional learning for HODs (research project). • Online modules with some face-to-face meetings dependent on COVID lockdowns. • Assessment shift (Approaches to Learning rubric introduced). • Co-wrote and published Association of Heads of Independent Schools of Australia (AHISA) magazine article. • Presented at Association of Independent Schools ACT Showcase.	• Secondary school staff (CoPs) and focus group. HODs continuously updated. • Student voice sessions – to seek feedback on experience to date. • Hosting visiting schools interested in school-wide approaches for SRL.	• Presentation of student focus group data analysis and findings. • Presentation at 2024 National Education Summit. • Presentation at the 2024 Research Conversation at St Andrews Cathedral School (postponed from 2023).

Launching a whole-school SRL initiative

Bonython Primary School formally started its SRL school improvement initiative in 2021; refer Table 41.

Table 41. Overview of Bonython Primary School's approach to SRL professional learning

2021 Establishing interest/value	2022 Learning and sharing	2023 Learning and sharing	2024 Learning and sharing
Teachers as researchers project – a small group of staff conducting an inquiry into SRL with Dr Shyam Barr as a critical friend.	Leadership Focus Group (initial year-long deep dive to ensure leaders were well-positioned to support staff). This involved three three-hour workshops per term for the whole year.	• Leadership Focus Group. • Leadership coaching. • All-staff professional education. • Teacher Focus Group. • Educator inquiries.	• Leadership Focus Group. • Leadership coaching. • All-staff professional education. • Teacher Focus Group. • Educator inquiries.

One element that is consistent and highly effective across both Radford College and Bonython Primary School is the role of regular feedback and communication cycles with all stakeholders. We'll look at that next.

Seek and share feedback about the SRL initiative

Seeking and sharing feedback from various stakeholders is pivotal for the success of a school improvement initiative. This process not only garners diverse perspectives but ensures that the initiative aligns with the needs and expectations of all involved parties, including staff, students, parents, community members and the program designers.

Flinders University's (2023) Sustaining Innovation Through Education (SITE) tool documents four different levels of gathering and disseminating feedback. For effective implementation, it is recommended that feedback on both the process of implementation and outcomes of the initiative be shared with staff, students, parents and other stakeholders at least annually. Sharing feedback with the program designer is equally important. It aids in refining the initiative based on real-world application and outcomes, ensuring that the program remains relevant and effective.

Feedback to different stakeholders can occur in different forms. Bonython Primary School uses a combination of approaches, including learning walls (refer Figure 25) to share and celebrate progress and outcomes with staff, and a Festival of Inquiry that incorporates educator inquiries about SRL (refer Figure 26).

Feedback plays a crucial role as it informs changes to the implementation processes, ensuring that the initiative continually evolves to meet students' changing needs. Documenting and communicating these adaptations, as well as analysing their success or failure, are essential steps in the feedback loop.

Figure 25. Bonython Primary School's SRL learning walls

Figure 26. Bonython Primary School's Festival of Inquiry

Bonython Primary School Educator Inquiry Artifacts (i.e. frames and booklets) displayed on a table, showcasing each teacher's personal research into SRL.

Acknowledge schools as complex adaptive systems

When planning and implementing an SRL school improvement initiative, keep in mind that schools are *complex adaptive systems* (Koh et al., 2023).

Schools are open systems consisting of multiple, different and interdependent subsystems, and are deeply integrated into real-world settings and influenced by myriad external factors. For instance, they are shaped by government policies, community expectations, and global trends. Internally, schools consist of diverse, interacting entities including different groups of students, teachers, administrators, and subsystems like curriculum and policies.

Schools are committed to ongoing improvement, a process that is dynamic and non-linear. This means that the relationship between actions taken and outcomes achieved can be disproportionate, illustrating what is known as the 'butterfly effect'. For example, significant interventions might lead to minor changes, while smaller initiatives could have substantial impacts. This concept, initially coined by meteorologist Edward Lorenz, reflects the unpredictable nature of inputs and outputs within complex systems.

Changes within schools are emergent, unpredictable and often transient. These changes arise from interactions within the school system and with the external educational environment. They are influenced by a variety of factors and feedback loops at multiple levels. Understanding these emergent changes, rather than pinpointing specific causes, provides a more holistic view of how schools as complex systems evolve and adapt.

When we understand schools as complex adaptive systems, we recognise that school improvement initiatives cannot exist as isolated initiatives – an initiative's survival is dependent on how it interacts with the different parts of the school, meaning that any SRL school improvement initiative must evolve through its interactions with the different parts. For example, as staff turnover occurs, professional education must adapt to allow different entry points for teacher-learners starting at different points in the journey. In one school I worked with, new staff were onboarded through a mentorship program that aligned with SRL principles, allowing experienced teachers to guide newcomers in integrating these strategies into their teaching. This not only maintained the continuity of SRL initiatives but ensured that the evolving dynamic of the staff body contributed to, rather than disrupted, the systemic growth of SRL within the school culture.

Steps to plan an SRL school improvement initiative

When planning your school improvement initiative about SRL, consider the prompts presented in Table 42.

By following the prompts listed in Table 42 you ensure that the initiative is well-positioned for sustainability within the school.

Table 42. An overview of the steps to planning a sustainable SRL school improvement initiative

Step	What effective leaders do
1. Assessing students' SRL needs	Use various methods to evaluate student SRL behaviours, such as competency-based assessments, surveys and focus groups, to determine the need for SRL instruction.

Step	What effective leaders do
2. Communicating the initiative	Explain the importance of SRL and why it's relevant now by: • sharing current data on student SRL • presenting research that supports SRL initiatives • showing how SRL aligns with the school's documents, values, and strategic plan • informing parents and other stakeholders via newsletters or online platforms.
3. Understanding current teaching practices	Investigate teachers' understanding and application of SRL through surveys, interviews, focus groups and observing lessons. This helps identify any gaps or misconceptions teachers may have about SRL.
4. Involving staff in strategic planning	• Include staff from various roles and departments in planning the SRL initiative. • Form a dedicated team to visibly lead the initiative. • Encourage distributed leadership to create shared ownership. • Value staff input on implementing SRL strategies.
5. Drafting a strategic plan	• Outline clear goals, implementation methods and evaluation processes for SRL. • Plan for the initiative's sustainability. • Consider funding requirements and communication of regular feedback. • Optionally, include SRL responsibilities in staff job descriptions or performance reviews to ensure accountability.
6. Sharing the long-term vision	• Communicate the overarching goals of the SRL initiative. • Discuss how it fits among other programs. • Ensure open communication with staff, students and other stakeholders about the initiative's progress and expectations.

ADAPTED FROM FLINDERS UNIVERSITY'S (2023) SUSTAINING INNOVATION THROUGH EDUCATION ONLINE ASSESSMENT TOOL.

Creating space for SRL teaching initiatives

One of the key challenges of teaching SRL is navigating the constraints of time and competing demands that educators face. The friction arises as teachers juggle numerous educational priorities, which can sideline the integration of SRL strategies into daily teaching practices. To mitigate these barriers, schools must address this at an organisational level, perhaps by streamlining curricular demands to create space for SRL instruction. You might consider several strategies:

- **Curricular auditing:** Evaluating the current curriculum to identify areas where SRL principles can be naturally integrated without adding extra content, thereby enriching existing lessons rather than overcrowding the curriculum.
- **Professional development:** Providing teachers with training that equips them to embed SRL strategies within the content they are already teaching, which can enhance the learning experience without requiring additional class time.
- **Policy adjustments:** Revising school policies to prioritise SRL, such as adjusting learning outcomes to include self-regulatory skills, which signals the value of SRL within the school culture.
- **Collaborative planning:** Encouraging team teaching and collaborative planning, where educators can share the responsibility of incorporating SRL strategies across subjects, distributing the workload more evenly.

By adopting these approaches, you can facilitate the incorporation of SRL into teaching practices in a manner that respects both the teachers' time and the myriad educational goals they must meet. Additionally, teachers should be reminded that:

- **The explicit teaching of SRL strategies is not time-intensive once mastered.** Educators might self-record their SRL strategy instruction to evaluate the actual time spent and refine the process.
- **The long-term benefits of implementing SRL outweigh the initial time investment.** Research shows that SRL not only enhances student learning outcomes but can also lead to more efficient classroom practices, as students become more proactive and independent in their learning journey.

Chapter summary

This chapter explored the importance of communicating a strong *why* for SRL as part of introducing an SRL initiative. We discussed the process of crafting a rich professional learning experience that incorporates different levels of learning, features various forms of professional learning experiences and is designed for longevity. Such a professional learning experience is optimised for long-lasting results, and when combined with other elements of sustainable school improvement for SRL, it positions your community to become self-regulated learners. By seeing the overview of steps to implementing a sustainable SRL school improvement initiative, you can see a path to developing a whole-school approach to promoting SRL.

Take action

- Plan an SRL professional learning experience that:
    - incorporates different levels of learning
    - features various forms of professional learning experiences
    - is designed for longevity.
- As you plan your SRL school improvement initiative, work through the steps in Table 42 as a checklist. Does your SRL initiative meet these quality recommendations?
- Support teachers to work in a group or pairs to prepare a lesson with a new SRL strategy. Invite them to try it out in multiple classes, generating feedback from students, or asking students to promote it with other students.

Delve deeper

My website **shyambarr.com/book** includes links to the following resources so you can explore the concepts in this chapter further.

- ☐ Revisit Evidence for Learning's Red Amber Green assessment tools for Teacher knowledge and practice and Whole-school approach to curriculum and teaching.
- ☐ Read Radford College's AHISA article as an example of a wider communication that celebrates the school's SRL improvement initiative.
- ☐ Consider the Flinders University Sustaining Innovation Through Education (SITE) online self-assessment tool as part of planning your SRL school improvement initiative.

What? So what? Now what? strategy

The What? So what? Now what? strategy, originally used as part of a critical incident model within health sciences (Rolfe, 2001), is a reflection model that offers a structured method to analyse learning experiences. This model is particularly conducive to SRL as it encourages learners to critically examine their actions (What?), the importance and outcomes of these actions (So what?), and to plan future actions based on this reflection (Now what?). The questions align with SRL's emphasis on metacognition, where students assess their own learning processes and outcomes (the SRL phase of evaluating), thereby fostering deeper learning and the ability to set goals and adapt strategies for future learning tasks (the SRL phase of planning).

Identify a recent event or activity relevant to the learning, teaching or leading of SRL. Reflect on the event by asking yourself the following questions:

- What… happened?
- So what… does this mean?
- Now what… will I/we do?

Write down your responses to structure your reflective practice.

Applying the strategy in the classroom

After a meeting, lesson or activity, explicitly teach the What? So what? Now what? strategy to your learners using the NEMO-T approach (described in Chapter 4). Lead participants through the reflective questions to help them achieve a deeper level of reflection on their learning. This could be a protocol to use as part of their learning journal.

Transfer to other contexts

In what other contexts could you use the What? So what? Now what? strategy to foster a deeper reflection. For example, consider how the strategy could be applied in the context of a leader reflecting on a critical incident at school, a learner reflecting and evaluating a sporting performance or an assessment outcome.

For a range of questions that extends the 'What? So What? Now What?' strategy, read the blog 'Enhance your reflective practice with this simple tool' via shyambarr.com/book.

Conclusion

> The long-term benefit for young people is that when they leave school, they haven't mastered a school system but a learning system that they can adapt to different contexts.
>
> — Dr Shyam Barr

Alex is convinced that to be truly transformative, her practice must encompass SRL. As a teacher, she now views her subject not as the be-all and end-all, but as a vehicle to teach students SRL skills. Furthermore, in collaborating with her colleagues, arguably effective teachers, they are in agreeance – there is a large and complex body of knowledge that underpins both SRL and the teaching of SRL, and to effectively foster this skill set in their young people, they too must delve deeper into this field. As a school leader, Alex sets off to help her school implement structures where more staff can access professional learning about SRL and where the school's vision, mission and policies reflect a consistent and aligned focus on supporting SRL.

In this book, similar to Alex's journey, we have explored the multifaceted nature of SRL and its critical importance in contemporary education. We started by defining SRL and discussing its significance, setting the foundation for a deeper understanding. Our journey then took us through various instructional approaches tailored to assess and develop students' SRL abilities, emphasising the integration of SRL strategies into curriculum design and pedagogy. We examined the impact of classroom climate on SRL and delved into the more formal assessment and reporting techniques that capture and communicate the essence of SRL competencies. The book culminated in a practical guide for initiating and leading school improvement efforts centred on SRL. As you read this final section, it is my hope that you carry forward the insights and strategies discussed here to foster a generation of self-regulated learners equipped to navigate the challenges of a dynamic world.

> **Imagine students planning, monitoring and evaluating their learning.**

You notice them being proactive in their learning efforts: setting challenging learning goals and selecting appropriate strategies to achieve their goals. They are making choices that support deep learning and they are reaping the benefits. They are aware of their strengths, but equally their limitations and are now carefully monitoring and evaluating their chosen strategies and subsequent learning. They are reflective learners and when they hit a stumbling block, they put it down to effort and strategy and adapt for greater progress. And, as they engage in SRL, they experience greater self-awareness, better retain information and achieve mastery of content in shorter periods of time. Indeed, your students now have a greater level of self-satisfaction and, therefore, motivation to engage in continuous improvement, which leads to higher academic achievement and increased optimism about their future (Zimmerman, 2002; Dignath et al., 2008).

> **They are self-regulated. They are self-managers. They are equipped with skills and a learning orientation that will serve them for life.**

As they enter the workforce, whether exploring a new technology, developing their communication skills or shadowing senior leaders, they can better self-regulate their learning process to bring about a higher level of success. They can effectively learn the requisite skills, but are also well-equipped to generate new knowledge or skills, positioning themselves as sought-after employees. As they self-regulate their learning in formal environments, some (hopefully all) may realise that SRL has applications in other areas of their life, such as how they self-regulate their learning about health, finance, spirituality, relationships and so on.

> **Imagine, as educators, having peace of mind knowing that your practice was carefully informed by the developing evidence base of cognitive psychology and SRL. You know that you are designing the best possible learning experiences for your students – to not just survive, but thrive in this rapidly changing world.**

As a result of helping your students to better self-regulate as learners, you feel chuffed, proud, joyful, relieved and happy (just to represent a few of the many positive feelings teachers have shared with me). Along with these positive feelings, you now find yourself spending less time regulating or co-regulating students' behaviour for learning (e.g. redirecting attention, 'putting out spot fires'), leaving you with more time to delve into deeper conversations about your content/subject area (your passion) and really support critical thinking, creativity and the other general capabilities. The richness of the conversations leads to better relationships with your students. No matter the size of your class, you can now focus on the real learning challenges that require attention rather than constantly addressing surface-level issues. In other words, by your students engaging in SRL, this alleviates the general classroom management activities that take up time – and you can make professional choices about how best to re-allocate that time to deeper learning activities. But, most of all, you can be confident that you have drawn on the best available evidence to inform your practice – the best decisions you can make with the information available to you.

References

ACARA. (2024). The Australian Curriculum. Accessed 22 February 2024. https://v9.australiancurriculum.edu.au/

ACT Education Directorate. (2018). *The future of education: An ACT education strategy for the next ten years*. Accessed 9 February 2024. https://www.education.act.gov.au/__data/assets/pdf_file/0015/1231080/Future-Of-Education-Final-Strategy_Web.pdf

Australian Institute for Teaching and School Leadership (AITSL). (n.d). 'Learning Intentions And Success Criteria.' Accessed 14 February 2024. https://www.aitsl.edu.au/docs/default-source/feedback/aitsl-learning-intentions-and-success-criteria-strategy.pdf

Bandura, A. (2001). Social cognitive theory: An agentic perspective. *Annual Review of Psychology*, 52, 1–26. https://doi.org/10.1146/annurev.psych.52.1.1

Barr, S. & Askell-Williams, H. (2020). Changes in teachers' epistemic cognition about self–regulated learning as they engaged in a researcher-facilitated professional learning community, Asia-Pacific Journal of Teacher Education, 48:2, 187–212. https://doi.org/10.1080/1359866X.2019.1599098

Barr, S. (2021). Sustainable school improvement: Enhancing school middle leaders' epistemic cognition for teaching about self-regulated learning [Doctor of Philosophy, Flinders University]. Flinders University Theses Collection. Accessed 15 February 2024. https://theses.flinders.edu.au/view/59eae961-da6f-42bd-9af4-f94f54bc28ef/1

Barr, S. (2022a). What we fail to learn in schools: Self-regulated learning. TED. Accessed 13 February 2024. https://www.ted.com/talks/shyam_barr_what_we_fail_to_learn_in_schools

Barr, S. (2022b). Diagnostic assessment of middle-leaders' thinking and practice at X School. Presentation at X School's Academic Executive Forum.

Bellhäuser, H., Dignath, C. and Theobald, M. (2023). Daily automated feedback enhances self-regulated learning: A longitudinal randomized field experiment. *Frontiers*. Accessed 22 February 2024. https://www.frontiersin.org/articles/10.3389/fpsyg.2023.1125873/full#ref53

Bernard, S., Proust, J., & Clement, F. (2015). Procedural Metacognition and False Belief Understanding in 3- to 5-Year-Old Children. *PLOS One*, 10(10): e0141321. https://doi.org/10.1371/journal.pone.0141321

Bouwer, R., Koster, M., & van den Bergh, H. (2018). Effects of a strategy-focused instructional program on the writing quality of upper elementary students in the Netherlands. *Journal of Educational Psychology*, 110(1), 58–71. https://doi.org/10.1037/edu0000206

Brown, A. L., Campione, J. C. & Day, J. C. (1981). Learning to learn: On training students to learn from text. *Educational Researcher*, 10(2), 14–21.

Bruning, R. H., Schraw, G. J., Norby, M. M., & Ronning, R. R. (2010). *Cognitive psychology and instruction* (5th ed.). Pearson.

Callan, G. L., Longhurst, D., Ariotti, A., & Bundock, K. (2020). Settings, exchanges, and events: The SEE framework of self-regulated learning supportive practices. *Psychology in the Schools, 58*(5), 773–788. https://doi.org/10.1002/pits.22468

Callan, G., Longhurst, D., Shim, S., & Ariotti, A. (2022). Identifying and predicting teachers' use of practices that support SRL. *Psychology in the Schools, 59*(11), 2327–2344. https://doi.org/10.1002/pits.22712

Chi, M. T. H., & Wylie, R. (2014). The ICAP Framework: Linking Cognitive Engagement to Active Learning Outcomes. *Educational Psychologist, 49*(4), 219–243. https://doi.org/10.1080/00461520.2014.965823

Chow, C. W., & Chapman, E. (2017). Construct Validation of the Motivated Strategies for Learning Questionnaire in a Singapore High School Sample. *Journal of Educational and Developmental Psychology, 7*(2), 107. https://doi.org/10.5539/jedp.v7n2p107

Cohen, J. (1992). A power primer. *Psychological Bulletin, 112*(1), 155–159. https://doi.org/10.1037/0033-2909.112.1.155

Council of Australian Governments Education Council. (2019). Alice Springs (Mparntwe) education declaration. Accessed 22 February 2024. https://www.education.gov.au/alice-springs-mparntwe-education-declaration

Council of the European Union. (2018). Council Recommendation of 22 May 2018 on key competences for lifelong learning. *Official Journal of the European Union*. https://eur-lex.europa.eu/legal-content/EN/TXT/?uri=uriserv:OJ.C_.2018.189.01.0001.01.ENG&toc=OJ:C:2018:189:TOC

Creswell, J. W., & Guetterman, T. C. (2019). *Educational Research: Planning, Conducting, and Evaluating Quantitative and Qualitative Research* (6th ed.). Pearson

Csikszentmihalyi, M. (2009) *Flow*. Harper Perennial.

Danziger, S., Levav, J. and Avnaim-Pesso, L. (2011). Extraneous factors in judicial decisions. *Proceedings of the National Academy of Sciences of the United States of America, 108*, 6889–6892. https://doi.org/10.1073/pnas.1018033108

Darmawan, I. G. N., Vosniadou, S., Lawson, M.J., Van Deur, P. & Wyra M. (2020). The development of an instrument to test pre-service teachers' beliefs consistent and inconsistent with self-regulation theory. *British Journal of Educational Psychology, 90*(4), 1039–1061. https://doi.org/10.1111/bjep.12345

De Smul, M., Heirweg, S., Van Keer, H., Devos, G., & Vandevelde, S. (2018). How competent do teachers feel instructing self-regulated learning strategies? Development and validation of the teacher self efficacy scale to implement self-regulated learning. *Teaching and Teacher Education, 71*, 214–225. http://doi.org/10.1016/j.tate.2018.01.001

Department of Education and Training (DET). 2020. High Impact Teaching Strategies: Excellence in teaching and learning. Accessed 14 February 2024. https://www.education.vic.gov.au/Documents/school/teachers/support/highimpactteachstrat.docx

Desimone, L. M. (2009). Improving impact studies of teachers' professional development: Toward better conceptualizations and measures. *Educational Researcher, 38*(3), 181–199. https://doi.org/10.3102/0013189X08331140

Desoete, R. & Roeyers, D. (2005). Cognitive skills in mathematical problem solving in Grade 3. *British Journal of Educational Psychology, 75*(1), 119–138.

Dignath, C., & Büttner, G. (2008). Components of fostering self-regulated learning among students. A meta-analysis on intervention studies at primary and secondary school level. *Metacognition and Learning, 3*(3), 231–264. https://doi.org/10.1007/s11409-008-9029-x

Dignath, C., & Büttner, G. (2018). Teachers' direct and indirect promotion of self-regulated learning in primary and secondary school mathematics classes – Insights from video-based classroom observations and teacher interviews. *Metacognition and Learning, 13*, 127–157. https://doi.org/10.1007/s11409-018-9181-x

Dignath-van Ewijk, C., Dickhäuser, O., & Büttner, G. (2013). Assessing How Teachers Enhance Self-Regulated Learning: A Multiperspective Approach. *Journal of Cognitive Education and Psychology, 12*(3), 338. https://doi.org/10.1891/1945-8959.12.3.338

Dignath, C., & Veenman, M. (2021). Metacognitive strategies in student learning: A comprehensive review. *Educational Psychology Review, 33*(4), 1149–1185. https://doi.org/10.1007/s10648-021-09599-7

Dignath, C., Biegel, M., Veenman, M., & Büttner, G. (2022). Assessing How Teachers Enhance Self-Regulated Learning (ATES) [Rating manual: Version 1.0]. Erstanwendung 2008. Frankfurt am Main: Forschungsdatenzentrum Bildung am DIPF. Accessed 15 February 2024. https://www.fdz-bildung.de/get_files.php?daqsfile_id=25190

Dignath, C., Büttner, G., & Langfeldt, H. P. (2008). How can primary school students learn self-regulated learning strategies most effectively? A meta-analysis on self-regulation training programs. Educational Research Review, 3(2), 101–129. https://doi.org/10.1016/j.edurev.2008.02.003

Dignath, C., van Ewijk, R., Perels, F., & Fabriz, S. (2023). Let learners monitor the learning content and their learning behavior! A meta-analysis on the effectiveness of tools to foster monitoring. *Educational Psychology Review, 35*(2), Article 62. https://doi.org/10.1007/s10648-023-09718-4

Dignath-van Ewijk, C., & van der Werf, G. (2012). What teachers think about self-regulated learning: Investigating teacher beliefs and teacher behavior of enhancing students' self-regulation. *Education Research International*, Article ID 741713, 1–11. https://doi.org/10.1155/2012/741713

Donker, A. S., De Boer, H., Kostons, D., Dignath-Van Ewijk, C. C., & Van der Werf, M. P. C. (2014). Effectiveness of learning strategy instruction on academic performance: A meta-analysis. *Educational Research Review, 11*, 1–26. https://doi.org/10.1016/j.edurev.2013.11.002

Du, J., Hew, K. F., & Liu, L. (2023). What can online traces tell us about students' self-regulated learning? A systematic review of online trace data analysis. *Computers & Education, 201*, 104828. https://doi.org/10.1016/j.compedu.2023.104828

Dunlosky, J., Rawson, K. A., Marsh, E. J., Nathan, M. J., & Willingham, D. T. (2013). Improving students' learning with effective learning techniques: Promising directions from cognitive and educational psychology. *Psychological Science in the Public Interest, 14*(1), 4–58. https://doi.org/10.1177/1529100612453266

Edwards, O. V., & Dai, T. (2023). Differential relations among expectancy, task value, engagement, and academic performance: The role of generation status. *Frontiers in Education, 7*, 1033100. https://doi.org/10.3389/feduc.2022.1033100

Eilam, B., & Reiter, S. (2014). Long-term self-regulation of biology learning using standard junior high school science curriculum. *Science Education, 98*(4), 705–737. https://doi.org/10.1002/sce.21124

Elhusseini, S. A., Tischner, C. M., Aspiranti, K. B., & Fedewa, A. L. (2022). A quantitative review of the effects of self-regulation interventions on primary and secondary student academic achievement. *Metacognition and Learning, 17*, 1117–1139. https://doi.org/10.1007/s11409-022-09311-0

Evidence for Learning. (n.d.). Metacognition and self-regulated learning. Accessed 16 February 2024. https://evidenceforlearning.org.au/education-evidence/guidance-reports/metacognition

Fischer, A., & Dignath, C. (2023). How do teachers promote self-regulation of learning when students need to learn at home? The moderating role of teachers' ICT competency. *Unterrichtswiss.* https://doi.org/10.1007/s42010-023-00191-0

Fishbach, A., & Choi, J. (2012). When thinking about goals undermines goal pursuit. *Organizational Behavior and Human Decision Processes, 118*(2), 99–107. https://doi.org/10.1016/j.obhdp.2012.02.003

Flinders University. (2023). The Sustainability of Effective Educational Initiatives (SEEI). Accessed 22 February 2024. https://sites.flinders.edu.au/seei/

Gonski, D., Arcus, T., Boston, K., Gould, V., Johnson, W., O'Brien, L., et al. (2018). *Through growth to achievement: Report of the review to achieve educational excellence in Australian schools*. Canberra: Commonwealth of Australia.

Händel, M., & Dresel, M. (2022). Structure, relationship, and determinants of monitoring strategies and judgment accuracy. An integrated model and evidence from two studies. *Learning and Individual Differences, 100*. https://doi.org/10.1016/j.lindif.2022.102229

Hattan, C., Alexander, P. A., & Lupo, S. M. (2023). Leveraging What Students Know to Make Sense of Texts: What the Research Says About Prior Knowledge Activation. *Review of Educational Research, 94*(1). https://doi.org/10.3102/00346543221148478

Hattie, J., & Timperley, H. (2007). The Power of Feedback. *Review of Educational Research, 77*(1). https://doi.org/10.3102/003465430298487

Heirweg, S., De Smul, M., Merchie, E., Devos, G., & Van Keer, H. (2022). The long road from teacher professional development to student improvement: A school-wide professionalization on self-regulated learning in primary education. *Research Papers in Education, 37*(6), 929–953. https://doi.org/10.1080/02671522.2021.1905703

Hulleman, C.S., Godes, O., Hendricks, B.L., & Harackiewicz, J.M. (2010). Enhancing interest and performance with a utility value intervention. *Journal of Educational Psychology, 102*, 880–895.

Institute of Coaching and Consulting Psychology. (2016). Workshop notes from the Professional Certificate in Coaching Psychology (PCCP) [Unpublished workshop notes].

International Baccalaureate Organization. (n.d.). Learning and Teaching [Primary and Secondary Years Programme]. Accessed 22 February 2024. https://www.ibo.org/

King, R. & McInerney, D. (2016). Do goals lead to outcomes or can it be the other way around?: Causal ordering of mastery goals, metacognitive strategies, and achievement. *British Journal of Educational Psychology, 86*(3), 296–312.

Kistner, S., Rakoczy, K., Otto, B., Klieme, E., & Büttner, G. (2015). Teaching learning strategies: The role of instructional context and teacher beliefs. *Journal for Educational Research Online, 7*(1), 176–197. https://doi.org/10.25656/01:11052

Koh, G. A., Askell-Williams, H., & Barr, S. (2023). Sustaining school improvement initiatives: Advice from educational leaders. *School Effectiveness and School Improvement, 34*(3), 298–330. https://doi.org/10.1080/09243453.2023.2190130

Lawson, M. J., Vosniadou, S., Van Deur, P., Wyra, M., & Jeffries, D. (2018). Teachers' and students' belief systems about the self-regulation of learning. *Educational Psychology Review, 31*, 223–251. https://doi.org/10.1007/s10648-018-9453-7

Lee, M., Lee, S. Y., Kim, J. E., & Lee, H. J. (2023). Domain-specific self-regulated learning interventions for elementary school students. *Learning and Instruction, 88*(101810). https://doi.org/10.1016/j.learninstruc.2023.101810

Leutwyler, B, & Maag Merki, K. (2009). School effects on students' self-regulated learning. *Journal for Educational Research Online, 1*, 197–223.

Liem, G.A., & Martin, A.J. (2012). The Motivation and Engagement Scale: Theoretical framework, psychometric properties, and applied yields. *Australian Psychologist, 47*, 3–13. https://doi.org/10.1111/j.1742-9544.2011.00049.x

Lombaerts, K., De Backer, F., Engels, N., van Braak, J., & Athanasou, J. (2009). Development of the Self-Regulated Learning Teacher Belief Scale. *European Journal of Psychology of Education, 24*(1), 79–96. http://www.jstor.org/stable/23421820

Markauskaite, L., Marrone, R., Poquet, O., Knight, S., Martinez-Maldonado, R., Howard, S., Tondeur, J., De Laat, M., Buckingham Shum, S., Gašević, D., & Siemens, G. (2022). Rethinking the entwinement between artificial intelligence and human learning: What capabilities do learners need for a world with AI? *Computers and Education: Artificial Intelligence, 3*. https://doi.org/10.1016/j.caeai.2022.100056

Martin, A. J. (2007). Examining a multidimensional model of student motivation and engagement using a construct validation approach. *British Journal of Educational Psychology, 77*, 413-440. https://doi.org/10.1348/000709906X118036

Martin, A. J. (2009). Motivation and engagement across the academic lifespan: A developmental construct validity study of elementary school, high school, and university/college students. *Educational and Psychological Measurement, 69*, 794–824. https://doi.org/10.1177/0013164409332214

Martin, A. J. (2023). Integrating motivation and instruction: Towards a unified approach in educational psychology. *Educational Psychology Review*, 35–54. https://doi.org/10.1007/s10648-023-09774-w

Martin, A. J., Guay, F., & Hau, K-T. (2019). The role of motivation and engagement in promoting literacy and numeracy. IAAP United Nations White Paper Series. New York: International Association of Applied Psychology (IAAP).

Matthews, J., & Wrigley, C. (2017). Design and design thinking in business and management higher education. *Journal of Learning Design, 10*(1), 41–54.

Muijs, D., & Bokhove, C. (2020). *Metacognition and Self-Regulation: Evidence Review*. London: Education Endowment Foundation.

Murdoch, K. (2015). *The Power of Inquiry*. Seastar.

Nückles, M., Schwonke, R., Berthold, K., & Renkl, A. (2004). The use of public learning diaries in blended learning. *Journal of Educational Media, 29*, 49–66.

OECD. (2019a). *Education 2030 curriculum content mapping: An analysis of the Netherlands curriculum proposal*. Accessed 9 February 2024. https://www.oecd.org/education/2030-project/contact/E2030_CCM_analysis_NLD_curriculum_proposal.pdf

OECD. (2019b). Skills for 2030. Retrieved from https://www.oecd.org/education/2030-project/teaching-and-learning/learning/learning-compass-2030/

Panadero, E. (2017). A review of self-regulated learning: Six models and four directions for research. *Frontiers in Psychology, 8*, Article 422. https://doi.org/10.3389/fpsyg.2017.00422

Panadero, E., Jonsson, A., Pinedo, L., et al. (2023). Effects of rubrics on academic performance, self-regulated learning, and self-efficacy: A meta-analytic review. *Educational Psychology Review, 35*, 113. https://doi.org/10.1007/s10648-023-09823-4

Perry, N. E., Lisaingo, S., Yee, N., Parent, N., Wan, X., & Muis, K. (2020). Collaborating with teachers to design and implement assessments for self-regulated learning in the context of authentic classroom writing tasks. *Assessment in Education: Principles, Policy & Practice, 27*(4), 416–443. https://doi.org/10.1080/0969594X.2020.1801576

Piasta, S. B., Dynia, J. M., Justice, L. M., Pentimonti, J. M., Kaderavek, J. N., & Schatschneider, C. (2010). Impact of professional development on preschool teachers' print references during shared read alouds: A latent growth curve analysis. *Journal of Research on Educational Effectiveness, 3*(4), 343–380. https://doi.org/10.1080/19345747.2010.482177

Pintrich, P. R. (1999). The role of motivation in promoting and sustaining self-regulated learning. *International Journal of Educational Research, 31*(6), 459–470. https://doi.org/10.1016/S0883-0355(99)00015-4

Pintrich, P. R., & De Groot, E. (1990). Motivational and self-regulated learning components of classroom academic performance. *Journal of Educational Psychology, 82*, 33–40.

Pintrich, P. R., Smith, D. A. F., Garcia, T., & McKeachie, W. J. (1991). A manual for the use of the Motivated Strategies for Learning Questionnaire (MSLQ). Ann Arbor: University of Michigan, National Center for Research to Improve Postsecondary Teaching and Learning.

Ritchhart, R., Church, M., & Morrison, K. (2011). *Making Thinking Visible: How to Promote Engagement, Understanding, and Independence for All Learners*. Jossey-Bass.

Roebers, C. M. (2017). Executive function and metacognition: Towards a unifying framework of cognitive self-regulation. *Developmental Review, 45*, 31–51. https://doi.org/10.1016/j.dr.2017.04.001

Rolfe, G. (2001). *Critical reflection for nursing and the helping professions: A user's guide*. Basingstoke: Palgrave Macmillan.

Rosenzweig, E. Q., Wigfield, A., & Eccles, J. S. (2019). Expectancy-value theory and its relevance for student motivation and learning. In K. A. Renninger & S. E. Hidi (Eds.), *The Cambridge handbook of motivation and learning* (pp. 617–644). Cambridge University Press. https://doi.org/10.1017/9781316823279.026

Roth, A., Ogrin, S., & Schmitz, B. (2016). Assessing self-regulated learning in higher education: A systematic literature review of self-report instruments. *Educational Assessment, Evaluation and Accountability, 28*, 225–250. https://doi.org/10.1007/s11092-015-9229-2

Sanford, K. (2023). Pedagogically hacking the system: Developing a competency-based digital portfolio. In Assessment of online learners: Foundations and applications for teacher education (pp. 187–205).

Schraw, G. & Dennison, R. S. (1994). Assessing metacognitive awareness. *Contemporary Educational Psychology, 19*, 460-475.

Sins, P. H. M., Van Dijk, A. M., Tolkamp, J., Berends, R., Vrieling-Teunter, E., Senders, C., Vermeulen, I., Mooren, A., Smetsers, J., De Boer, M., Kroes, H., Snel, W., Van Heusden, M., Melody, E., Bussink, M., De Lange, A., Schemkes, H., Lubbers, A., & Hessels, M. (2019). *iSELF: Aanpak voor het bevorderen van zelfsturend leren door leraren* (2de editie) [iSELF: An approach for teaching self-regulated learning (2nd edition)]. Saxion Progressive Education.

Sins, P., de Leeuw, R., de Brouwer, J., & Vrieling-Teunter, E. (2023). Promoting explicit instruction of strategies for self-regulated learning: Evaluating a teacher professional development program in primary education. *Metacognition and Learning*. https://doi.org/10.1007/s11409-023-09368-5

Smith, T. E., Thompson, A. M., & Maynard, B. R. (2022). Self-management interventions for reducing challenging behaviors among school-age students: A systematic review. *Campbell Systematic Reviews, 18*(1), Article e1223. https://doi.org/10.1002/cl2.1223

Theobald, M. (2021). Self-regulated learning training programs enhance university students' academic performance, self-regulated learning strategies, and motivation: A meta-analysis. *Contemporary Educational Psychology, 66*(1), Article 101976. https://doi.org/10.1016/j.cedpsych.2021.101976

Tibbetts, Y., Canning, E. A., & Harackiewicz, J. M. (2015). Academic Motivation and Performance: Task Value Interventions. In J. D. Wright (Ed.), *International Encyclopedia of the Social & Behavioral Sciences* (2nd ed., pp. 37–42). Elsevier. https://doi.org/10.1016/B978-0-08-097086-8.26078-9

Veenman, M. V. (2017). Assessing metacognitive deficiencies and effectively instructing metacognitive skills. *Teachers College Record, 119*(13), 20. https://doi.org/10.1177/016146811711901303

Veenman, M. V. J., Van Hout-Wolters, B. H. A. M., & Afflerbach, P. (2006). Metacognition and learning: conceptual and methodological considerations. *Metacognition and Learning, 1*(1), 3–14. https://doi.org/10.1007/s11409-006-6893-0

Vosniadou, S., Lawson, M. J., Stephenson, H., & Bodner, E. (2021). Teaching students how to learn: Setting the stage for lifelong learning. International Academy of Education & UNESCO International Bureau of Education. Accessed 15 February 2024. https://unesdoc.unesco.org/ark:/48223/pf0000378839

Vosniadou, S., Lawson, M. J., Wyra, M., Van Deur, P., Jeffries, D., & Darmawan, I. G. N. (2020). Pre-service teachers' beliefs about learning and teaching and about the self-regulation of learning: A conceptual change perspective. *International Journal of Educational Research, 99*, 101495. https://doi.org/10.1016/j.ijer.2019.101495

Wang, J. (2012). Revised Motivated Strategies for Learning Questionnaire for Secondary School Students. *The International Journal of Research and Review, 8*, 19.

Whitebread, D., Coltman, P., Pasternak, D. P., Sangster, C., Grau, V., Bingham, S., Almeqdad, Q., & Demetriou, D. (2009). The development of two observational tools for assessing metacognition and self-regulated learning in young children. *Metacognition and Learning, 4*(1), 63–85.

Wigfield, A., and Eccles, J. S. (2020). 35 years of research on students' subjective task values and motivation: a look back and a look forward. In A. Elliot (Ed.), *Advances in motivation science* (Vol. 7, pp. 161–198). Elsevier Academic Press.

William, D. (2017). *Embedded Formative Assessment: Strategies for Classroom Assessment that Drives Student Engagement and Learning.* Bloomington, Indiana: Solution Tree.

William, D., and S. Leahy. (2015). *Embedding Formative Assessment: Practical Techniques for K-12 Classrooms.* West Palm Beach, FL: Learning Sciences International.

Woods, M. (2009). ALARM – A Learning and Responding Matrix. Accessed 16 February 2024. https://www.alarmeducation.com.au/

World Economic Forum. (2021). *Building a common language for skills at work: A global taxonomy.* Accessed 7 February 2024. https://www.weforum.org/publications/building-a-common-language-for-skills-at-work-a-global-taxonomy/

World Economic Forum. (2023). *The Future of Jobs Report 2023.* Accessed 22 February 2024. https://www.weforum.org/publications/the-future-of-jobs-report-2023/

Wu, B. & Goff, W. (2023). Learning intentions: a missing link to intentional teaching? Towards an integrated pedagogical framework. *Early Years, 43*:2, 411–425. , https://doi.org/10.1080/09575146.2021.1965099

Xu, Z., Zhao, Y., Liew, J., Zhou, X., & Kogut, A. (2023). Synthesizing research evidence on self-regulated learning and academic achievement in online and blended learning environments: A scoping review. *Educational Research Review, 39* (100510). https://doi.org/10.1016/j.edurev.2023.100510

Yoon, K. S., Duncan, T., Lee, S. W. Y., Scarloss, B., & Shapley, K. L. (2007). Reviewing the evidence on how teacher professional development affects student achievement. Washington DC: U.S. Department of Education, Institute of Education Sciences, National Center for Education Evaluation and Regional Assistance, Regional Educational Laboratory Southwest. Accessed 22 February 2024. https://ies.ed.gov/ncee/edlabs/regions/southwest/pdf/rel_2007033.pdf

Zimmerman, B. J., & Schunk, D. H. (2011). Self-regulated learning: An introduction and an overview. In B. J. Zimmerman & D. H. Schunk (Eds.), *Handbook of self-regulated learning and performance* (pp. 1–12). Routledge.

About the author

Dr Shyam Barr is dedicated to guiding individuals on their journey to becoming self-regulated learners. With a background as a secondary school teacher and educational leader, he now advances the field of SRL as a Professional Associate at the University of Canberra's Faculty of Education and, prior to this, as an Assistant Professor of Learning Sciences. His research explores school improvement initiatives and evidence-informed teaching approaches for fostering students' SRL in classrooms.

Shyam has achieved multiple awards for educational innovation and secured various industry-research grants to advance research in teaching SRL. His educational qualifications are extensive. He holds both a Bachelor of Education and a Bachelor of Science with a major in Psychology. He has attained two Master of Education degrees, specialising in Leadership, Policy and Change, and Cognitive Psychology and Educational Practice, respectively. His scholarly pursuits culminated in 2021 with the award of a Doctor of Philosophy (PhD) for his thesis 'Sustainable school improvement: Enhancing school middle-leaders epistemic cognition for teaching about SRL'.

As an active voice in educational discourse, Shyam co-hosts the podcast *Educate to Self-Regulate*, aimed at educational leaders, teachers and students. He has been a guest on numerous educational local and international podcasts, educational panels about the future of skills and the role of SRL and has also shared his insights as a speaker at TEDx Canberra 2022, extending his impact in the field.

Shyam works with schools and educators in a variety of capacities, including speaking and workshops, school partnerships and coaching and mentoring. For help with promoting students' SRL, get in touch with Dr Shyam Barr via shyambarr.com.

www.ingramcontent.com/pod-product-compliance
Lightning Source LLC
Chambersburg PA
CBHW050357120526
44590CB00015B/1718